basis for improved accomplishment. In suggesting that musical talent, in a wider sense, is universal and that most people are sufficiently talented to play a musical instrument well, he brings to the reader a new sense of encouragement about performance possibilities and his own abilities as a performer or listener.

Throughout the book, to clarify his points, Dr. Barnett makes apt comparisons between music and poetry, drama, photography, sports, and various everyday activities. All technical terms are explained as they first appear in the text and defined in a glossary at the back. All examples are drawn from music playable on the piano.

As a complete rationale of musical performance, this practical handbook of interpretation will be read with interest, enjoyment, and instruction not only by teachers, students, and composers of music and by musical amateurs but also by teachers and students of pyschology, philosophy, and esthetics.

THE AUTHOR: As a solo pianist David Barnett has given concerts and lecture recitals in the United States and Europe, as well as on television, has appeared with the Boston, Cincinnati, St. Louis, and Paris symphony orchestras, and has made recordings. His music is published by Associated Music Publishers, Oxford University Press, and Salabert. He has contributed articles to music education journals and to *Vogue*, and he is the author of three previous books, *Living with Music*, *They Shall Have Music*, and *Manual for Grade Teachers*. Dr. Barnett has taught at Wellesley College, Harvard and Columbia universities, and the New England Conservatory of Music, and he is presently Professor of Music at the University of Bridgeport.

The Performance of Music

A Study in Terms of the Pianoforte

DAVID BARNETT

UNIVERSE BOOKS
New York

TO MY WIFE JOSEPHINE
AND MY SON JONATHAN

Published in the United States of America in 1972
by Universe Books
381 Park Avenue South, New York, N.Y. 10016
Copyright in 1972 in all countries
of the International Copyright Union
by Universe Books. All rights reserved,
including the right of
reproduction in whole or in part.
Library of Congress Catalog Card Number: 70-172483
Universe Books ISBN 0-87663-155-3
Printed in Great Britain

CONTENTS

VI   The Definition of Musical Talent

I A GENERAL VIEW OF THE FACTORS IN PERFORMANCE

INTRODUCTION

This book is about a musical trinity—the composer, the performer, and the listener. Unlike the Trinity of Christianity, it has not been closely studied as a concept. Yet, due to a curious, paradoxical circumstance, it is extremely subtle and complicated. The three members seem to act independently while each must certainly be keeping the others in mind. The composer expects his structure to stand like a building by itself, yet his music must be possible to perform and understandable when heard. The performer also creates his own edifice of sound, yet it is the outcome of the composer's work and is judged by its effect on the listener. The listener's experience depends on his own musical capacity and system of associations, yet they are brought into play by the powers of the performance and by the composition being interpreted. All three activities are at once autonomous and overlapping, and in many successful performances one often cannot decide which was most responsible—beautifully constructed music, penetrating interpretation, or perceptive listening.

Under such circumstances, disputes can easily arise over the roles the three members are to play and the credit each is to receive. The composer can claim that, without his structure, performance and listening are impossible. The performer can maintain that, without his intervention, the composition remains silent. The listener can hold that, without his attention, the work of composer and performer is fruitless. Or each may shift the blame for a fiasco to the others: The music was poorly written or badly played, or the listeners were uneducated. These attitudes are typical, and there was probably no epoch in the history of music when composers did not complain about lack of rehearsal, when performers did not consider the demands upon them impossible, and when listeners were not castigated for low taste and fickleness. However, the present situation is unprecedented. Not simply do we hear the same complaints but the very function of each of the three members is being scrutinized and questioned. It is no longer a case of locating boundaries but of discussing whether there should be any boundaries at all. There is even talk about eliminating the performer, and, in an age when science is busy catching up with science fiction, one has little difficulty imagining something called music being transmitted by computers to electrodes that have been attached to the listener.

For those who still wish to live and work in the present, the problems have been aggravated. Amid the dissent and argument over the future of music, children must still be introduced to their musical heritage, music students must learn to play and to compose for existing instruments, and listeners who derive pleasure and profit from music of the past must be helped. A musical generation cannot be brought up in terms of what music may or may not become. If they are to lead their musical lives, it is necessary to disentangle conflicting strands and clarify what up to now have been functions and methods of composer, performer, and listener.

The purpose of this book, then, is to inquire into the intricate relationships among the three modes of participating in musical experience. We will find that while there is indeed an order of priority—the performer carries what the composer begins to its goal in the listener—all three are equally important. We will be surprised to discover that the composer directs his efforts much more to the listener than has ordinarily been thought and much less to the performer: he considers the performer akin to himself, as at the sending, not the receiving, end of the process. It will become evident that musical form and continuity owe their nature much more to the conditions of comprehension during listening than to abstract principles of construction.

For this reason, for the reason that the listener is both the object and the determinant of musical expression, I have decided to address this book to the general reader rather than to those whose interest in music is technical. I realize that this decision makes unusual demands on him and creates hardships for his attention. But my experience in music, curiously enough, fits me to be helpful in these difficulties. I have been as interested to work with amateurs as with students pursuing advanced degrees and have divided my teaching equally among them. In so doing, too, I have found that there was no need to dilute the intensity of my musical approach for the amateurs. They were entirely capable of understanding and discussing basic, subtle concepts of music provided that they were sufficiently encouraged and were not intimidated by technical terms. After all, the universality of music is of crucial importance to its well being, and those who would restrict music to themselves, under a halo of technical abstractions, only harm themselves as much as the art.

I have also decided to center my discussion on the pianoforte and to choose examples from its literature. My reasons are that it is the predominant instrument among amateurs; it draws the most students at colleges, conservatories, and music schools; it is frequently studied as a second instrument by players of other instruments; it offers the most practical means of reducing instrumentation for study purposes; in contrast to string instruments, it has been retained for a variety of purposes by composers and players of popular music.[1] Also, there is a technical advantage for Chapter III, which deals with the scientific evaluation of performances. Since the piano is an instrument with fixed pitch—that is, fixed in advance by the tuner and not created by the performer—I am able to reduce the discussion of the components of tone to more manageable proportions. Having composed for and played for other instruments, I am confident that my conclusions about piano performance apply to them as well, and I do not hesitate to suggest to other instrumentalists that they test what I illustrate through the piano in the light of their varieties of musical experience.

1 THE NEED FOR GREATER UNDERSTANDING OF PERFORMANCE

At some time between the First and Second World Wars, the attitude toward musical performance underwent a fundamental change. Of Ignaz Jan Paderewski, who made his American debut in 1891 and for forty years thereafter gave concerts throughout the United States, Richard Aldrich, the critic of *The New York Times*, wrote: "Mr. Paderewski's achievements were of a different and a higher sort, more deeply grounded in the nobility, the poetry, the pure artistic quality of his musicianship. He touched the deepest and tenderest feelings and tugged irresistibly at the heart-strings of a whole people."[2] By 1949, in a Charles Eliot Norton lecture at Harvard University, the composer Paul Hindemith could say to an audience that was quite prepared for his comment: "Once we accept the performer as an inevitable necessity in spite of his basic dubiousness, we may as well try to determine what properties make him estimable."[3]

The content of Hindemith's lectures shows that he was not being facetious, as one might expect of a violist of considerable eminence turned composer. It signified an attack on the status of the performer that had been going on for some time and from several directions. Apparently, the performer had monopolized musical glory. He was said to receive large sums for playing music that the composer, who was paid relatively little, had supplied. Furthermore, added the historian or musicologist, his performances were of doubtful authenticity. They showed little comprehension of styles, and the very emotionalism that so moved the audience was out of place. Finally, psychologists joined in, not so much to belittle the performer—their investigations were often prompted by admiration—as to show that his effect on audiences was not mysterious at all and could be explained by science.[4]

Under this triple attack, any monopoly of musical glory by the performer was broken. His status was considerably lowered and that of the composer, the historian, and the psychologist correspondingly raised. To perform music, the player had now to share the applause with the composer, pass the historian's tests for authenticity, and defer to the psychologist's contention that the effects he produced were largely illusory. It was of little avail to point out that the performers who were well paid were a small minority, that the quest for authenticity had many obstacles to overcome, and that the conclusions of the psychologists were being questioned even within their own field.

Inevitably, the type of performance began to change.[5] Like an unruly stream that has been tamed into a placid canal, it began to conform to these restrictive influences. But since there is something about performance itself that is unsuited to such restriction—performance, unlike composition, musicology, and psychology, involves physical activity, verve, and the immediacy of presentation to an audience—the effort to conform became painfully evident. The deference to the composer was forced and self-conscious and resulted in a substitution of artificial effect for natural expression. The subservience to the historian led to carrying out the markings of notation in literal fashion, in the interests of so-called fidelity to the printed page. And the uneasy awareness of the psychologist's scientific criteria caused a separation of accuracy, as a desirable objective in itself, from its normal, incidental relation to a job well done.

If this kind of performance were satisfying to either the performer or the listener, there would be nothing further to say.

But in uncomfortable reaction to the restrictions, the performer viewed the music page more and more as a series of explicit tasks; there was little else left to him but to concentrate on increasing the skill to carry them out. It is true that the listener is greatly impressed by skill, but unfortunately he quickly tires of it. He takes the same attitude as he does to a juggler. He forgets the feats he has just admired when the next act comes on. He has fallen into the habit of listening to one performer with the feeling that the next one may be even more astounding.

The emphasis on skill created other disadvantages as well. It placed one performer in more direct competition with another—that is, since skill is naturally more widespread than individuality, it created many more competitors than each might otherwise have had. Where competition of this sort is the rule, there will always be a fearful waste of human resources. The young performer practices for many years, makes his presentation, may even enjoy momentary recognition. Then, by the process of elimination, he is relegated to a teaching position for which he is not properly trained and from which, presumably, he will prepare younger students to go through the same cycle. Furthermore, competition on the basis of skill alienates the less skillful from participation in music. Even when concert performance is not the object, they find little attraction in the prospect of overcoming others who are already further along on the same road.[6]

Finally, the increased skill of performances has not increased the size of audiences to a corresponding extent. Indeed, it has helped to convince large sections of the populace that the musical masterpieces of the past are not meant for everyone. There have been wholesale desertions to the opposite camp of popular music, to a kind of music that does not require so long and arduous a preliminary. Underestimating the deterrent effect that the emphasis on skill has had, music educators, instead of reducing it, have sought to come to terms with the deserters. The optimists among them still think of popular music as a springboard to classical music, while the pessimists have begun to hail it as the music of the future.

Had the drastic change in attitude toward the performer been the result of new insights into the nature of performance, it might have been justified. But it was largely due to a re-distribution of power, a reshuffling of the forces governing the dissemination of music. What had aroused envy of the per-former was a relatively recent improvement in his status that dated from the advent of Liszt and Paganini (born in 1811 and 1782, respectively). These two virtuosi had a profound effect not only on the musically untrained masses who had been brought into the concert hall by the revolutionary movements at the end of the 18th century but on the cognoscenti as well. As Alfred Einstein points out in *Music in the Romantic Era*, "this was a new order of things, in which the artist, and particularly the composer, exercised a more or less high-priestly power." He quotes Liszt who exhorted all musicians "to raise and ennoble the position of artists through abolition of the abuses and injustices with which they are faced, and to take the necessary steps to preserve their dignity."[7] By "artist," Liszt meant both the composer and the performer, because he saw no distinction between the two. They were two activities of the same person (this was actually the general practice at the time), the performer being the spokesman, the all-important immediate contact with the public, for the composer's efforts to exalt the significance both of music and of musicians.

There had always been virtuosi, but the 19th century was an age of virtuosity.[8] Besides, the masses were involved more directly than ever before. Consequently, the attack on the per-former's status in the 1920s and '30s was also a condemnation of 19th-century virtuosity—Paderewski was one of the last examples—and of the attitude of the masses who supported it. The basis of this condemnation was mainly intellectual.

"Intellectual"—the word thus used to characterize a critical attitude toward the 19th century—is a rueful reminder that it was that century which turned musicians into intellectuals.

When Debussy spoke out against the large proportions to which Berlioz and Wagner had brought musical expression, he was profiting from a tradition established by Schumann, Berlioz, Liszt, and Wagner, namely, the right of the musician to adopt an intellectual attitude to his art. In other words, the musician was free to deliver critical judgments on his contemporaries and predecessors rather than leave these solely to professional critics and philosophers. Debussy, then, in denouncing the projection of grandiose works for vast orchestras and immense choruses and in calling for a return to subtlety, refinement, and a feeling for the miniature,[9] was in reality using the intellectual prerogative against the very men who had obtained that prerogative. But the unfavorable comparisons of the 19th to earlier centuries that Debussy made in the 1890s were mild indeed compared to the extreme and rabid diatribes of thirty years later. A reform movement, begun by Beethoven with his revolt against the patronage system and continued by Liszt with his efforts to improve the position of the musician, ended in the 1920s with a bitter, intellectual rejection of its outcome. The 19th century had merely replaced patronage by the nobility with patronage by the masses; the aristocracy, at least, was musically trained and properly disposed toward desirable artistic qualities.

From this brief review of pioneer efforts in the musician's behalf, we can now see why the change in attitude toward the performer has confused both his status and his task. The confusion has arisen from the desire to hold on to all the gains in the position of the musician that the 19th century had made while condemning the qualities and points of view that had brought them about. Clearly, the crucial factor in the situation has been the musical public. The 19th-century performers had satisfied the masses; somehow, in the words of Aldrich, they had been able to "tug irresistibly at the heart-strings of a whole people." The fact is that those who would surround the performer with restrictions have not been able to show how he is to regain the ear of the masses. Their idea has been to educate the masses to appreciate the restricted kind of performance that they advocate. It has not succeeded despite most energetic efforts in the schools, colleges, and communications media. No real contact with the musical public has been established to compare with the one that previously existed, and it will never be established while the performer is to follow the watchword that some of the more extreme partisans of restricted performance have coined for him: "Let the score speak for itself."[10]

The phrasing of this watchword was unfortunate. Certainly some performers had been guilty of taking unnecessary and undesirable liberties with the composer's score. But phrased in this way, what should have been a warning against tampering with the text was distorted into a notion that the score could actually speak for itself. A whole new approach to performance was based upon this notion and drew many supporters. Like the "deadpan" school of acting, it consisted in trying to play with as little interpretation and expression as possible. Obviously, the moment that the music page is turned into sound, the performer is interpreting whether he thinks so or not. The result may be as unemotional or expressionless as he wishes, but it is an interpretation nevertheless. As Hindemith acidly remarked, the performer is an "inevitable necessity," and without his intervention the score is dumb. For better or worse, it cannot speak for itself.

That so palpably false and misleading a notion could influence a style of performing is further evidence of the confusion surrounding the activity of performance. To find a way out, to dispel the clouds of confusion, there is great need for more understanding of performance itself. The question, What is performance? must be asked, as the question, What is art? was asked many times in the past. It is a time for re-examination of basic principles, for redetermination of the relation of the composer, the historian, and the psychologist to performance. This is a time, too, for redefinition of musical talent so that many students who have been alienated from performance can return to it with confidence. Musical ability is surprisingly widespread[11] and, provided that performance is not construed solely as concert performance, it could be utilized to great advantage. It could create a body of players who would be able to read and interpret music as people now read books. Instead of despairingly imitating concert performance, they would form a sounding board for new music, and they would know what to look for in the performances of the professionals.

2 THE SCORE AS A SCRIPT

To discuss the question, What is performance? will require the entire course and scope of this book. But it will be helpful at this point to outline some of the ideas that will be treated in detail in the succeeding chapters. To begin with, one must understand what the musical score is. It is a script, like the script for a play. The playwright gives no precise directions about the makeup that the actor is to apply, about the tone of his voice and the inflection of his speech, or about his movements and gestures on the stage. In the same way, the composer makes no attempt to prescribe how loud or soft or accented the notes should be, how long a time a hold or a ritard or an acceleration should take, or what qualities or timbres the notes should have. All these matters and many more are left to the performer to decide.

Musical performance, then, is an effort, an attempt by one or more players to interpret the musical composition on the basis of its script or score. A performance is not the score but simply one idea of it. Since no two performances are alike, there are as many ideas of the score as there are performances. On the one hand, a consensus about a given score acts to limit the extent to which performances of it differ. For example, a passionate interpretation of Debussy's Mélisande, along the lines of Wagner's conception of Isolde, would be considered to depart from the consensus about Debussy's opera. On the other hand, since a performance is an opinion and opinions differ, intense controversies may arise, as, for example, over how much ornament may be added to certain slow movements of Mozart or to certain preludes of Bach. Whether a performance falls within or beyond the consensus, the composer is completely dependent upon his performer. He awaits a verdict and, even when he is well established, it can go against him, at least temporarily. Wagner, in an interesting passage, described such a situation in the case of Beethoven's Ninth Symphony:

> Where formerly I had seen nothing but mystic constellations and soundless magical shapes, there now was poured out, as from innumerable springs, a stream of inexhaustible and heart-compelling melody ... It was the inexpressible effect of the Ninth Symphony, performed in a way I had hitherto had no notion of, that gave real life to my new-won old spirit.[12]

Wagner's change of heart about the Ninth Symphony, as a result of an illuminating performance, teaches us what the limits of criticism are, and also explains why it is so important for each listener to form his own opinion. The composer's score offers the framework for an infinite number of performances without at the same time prescribing the one definitive performance that all others should follow or imitate. Consequently, when a critic does not like a performance, this means that he performs the score differently, either actually or in imagination, or that he has heard a different performance that he prefers. He docs not have access to the authority of the composer precisely because the composer himself cannot authorize a single, definitive performance and would be well advised not to attempt it. For example, Rachmaninov, who was as excellent a pianist as he was a composer, recorded his own interpretations of his concerti and etudes. Were performers to imitate his recordings slavishly, his music would soon cease to be performed and die. It is the possibility of finding new meaning in works of the past that makes them a heritage.

3 THE FUNCTION OF NOTATION

Once we recognize that every performance is an interpretation based on the musical script or score, we are in a position to understand the function of notation. Notation, the term given to the symbols that make up the score, is defined in Grove's Dictionary as "the art of expressing musical ideas in writing."[13] Notice that there is no mention of the performer whatsoever, no reference to explicit tasks that the performer is to carry out. Yet these are the very reasons why the definition is correct and valuable. One might perhaps object to the use of the word "ideas," because its meaning for ordinary thinking does not

FIG. 1
Rondo, Piano Concerto No. 1 in D minor, Op. 15, by Brahms

offer a clear parallel to music. A better wording might be: "Notation is the art of detailing the processes of musical composition in written symbols." But any definition that sees notation as a series of instructions to the performer mistakes its function completely.

Why must we be so careful to eliminate the performer from the definition of notation? Because each notation symbol serves more than one purpose *at the same time*. The significance of this fact has not been sufficiently recognized. In Fig. 1, measures 1 to 4 of the Rondo from Brahms's Piano Concerto No. 1 in D minor, Op. 15, for example, the first note or symbol serves all the following purposes: it begins the movement (one might ordinarily expect such a note to be an upbeat); it is an eighth note (quaver) followed by a quarter note (crochet) and an eighth note, thus creating a syncopated rhythmic pattern; it is part of two-quarter time, *Allegro non troppo*; it commences a phrase lasting four measures and a melody lasting eight; it is in counterpoint with a melody in the bass; it has the pitch of A immediately below middle C; it is the fifth tone of the D minor scale; it represents the dominant harmony in conjunction with the first note of the bass; it is marked forte; it has a *staccato* dot; and it is scored for piano solo (although not exclusively, since the violins will repeat the same theme beginning with the ninth bar).

What an extraordinary power to condense! By means of a single symbol, notation can bring into play a dozen processes having to do with tonality, harmony, meter, rhythmic pattern, counterpoint, form, texture, and instrumentation. With two lines and a colored-in circle, it places all this information at the disposal of the player so that he can make a proper judgment of how to perform the note. Had the purpose been simply instruction—to play A below middle C strongly, shorter than an eighth note in two-quarter time at not too fast a tempo—he would be at a loss to know what to do. His area of choice would become too large, and his decision would be at the mercy of either whim or convenience.

4   The Place of Rote Learning

Thus, the performer's decisions are made, not according to instructions received directly from notation, but from the information it supplies concerning the compositional processes utilized by the composer. Yet we must not overlook important additional factors that figure in making these decisions. Among these are rote learning and what we shall call, and later discuss in detail, *conversance with idiom*. Notation evolved into its present form by a long, arduous process. Decisive steps toward its essential features were taken as late as the 11th century and important matters were still being debated in the 17th. The earlier function of notation, therefore, was to remind the performer of what he had already learned by rote in training schools. This function could remain adequate as long as music was homophonic or unaccompanied melody and under the training schools' control. With the development of many-voiced or polyphonic music, and when particular compositions came to be performed in distant cities or even nations, the function of notation had to be changed to its present one of detailing compositional processes. Nevertheless, the earlier rote stage survives in the fact that all musical learning commences by rote and with the single line or melody. The child performs before he can read, and this circumstance gives to imitation both its status and its importance.

Rote learning, then, played a key role in the history of performance and continues to do so in the musical training of children. But obviously, one cannot imitate sounds without first hearing them either consciously or unconsciously. Where language is concerned, the parents insist that the child listen consciously so that he can speak as soon as possible. No such urgency exists for music, and most listening to music is unconscious. Yet it has a definite effect. Like an unorganized Muzak, the sounds and rhythms of music are poured into the ears of people from childhood on, in school and church, on radio and television, at parades and dances and other community events. As the history of music shows, these sounds and rhythms change from epoch to epoch, so that a practiced ear can hear unfamiliar music and detect to which epoch it belonged. They constitute a prevailing idiom, and even the untrained people of the epoch develop a conversance with them and an expectation of their characteristic features before a note is played. The 18th century expected to hear the minuet, whereas the 19th did not and instead anticipated the waltz. Conversance with idiom, therefore, is an *oral supplement* to musical notation which greatly simplifies its task and the task of the composer as well.

5 Acceptance and Rejection of Notation Symbols

The time arrives when a musical epoch ends and a new idiom begins to replace the old. That is the moment when the capacity of notation to detail newly developed processes of composition is put to the test. Conversance with the new idiom's features does not yet exist, and, since relatively few musicians are employing these features, rote performance is not possible. At such times, the symbols of notation experience strain. Questions are raised about whether notation symbols in their existing form can express what the composer wishes to say. Proposals are made to alter them or to add new symbols. But these proposals are examined in the light of a very significant law. No new symbols will be accepted into notation that cannot be traced to the introduction of new compositional processes. The needs of the composer, not those of the performer, have decided the course of notation's evolution.

The notation symbol *crescendo* offers a good illustration of the operation of this law. It came into general use by the end of the 18th century as a result of changes in musical style. J. S. Bach had based his music on the harmonic progressions of the *continuo* (a standardized series of chords) and had linked his measures closely by means of motif connections. Mozart had contrasted short sections in balanced, symmetrical arrangements. Beethoven, in contrast to Bach and Mozart, often built phrase upon phrase by means of sequences in rising pitch, and this striking feature of his style generated a new feeling of excitement which in performance called for steadily increasing volume or the *crescendo* effect. A *crescendo* is inappropriate unless the structure of the music demands it, and that is why it can play no significant role in the works of Bach and Mozart. The composer must build the need for it into his structure, and when he does this he can be so confident that the performer will carry it out suitably that he places the word *crescendo* rather vaguely on the printed page without any indication of how much of a *crescendo* to make.[14]

That notation symbols are designed for the composer and not for the performer may be verified from an opposite point of view: Composers are either indifferent or hostile to symbols that are introduced for the performer's benefit. An example of a symbol that truly instructs the performer is the metronome mark. Introduced into notation after Maelzel's modification of the metronome in 1816, the metronome mark designates the duration of a given note value in fractions of a minute. The indication, quarter note equals 60, means that a quarter note has a duration of one second and the other note values are to be calculated accordingly. Nothing could be more explicit. Yet, the metronome mark did not succeed in replacing the Italian tempo marks, such as *allegro*, *andante*, *lento*, which are notation symbols of great complexity as well as of considerable interpretive significance.

Composers who did use metronome marks—Brahms largely ignored them, Ravel employed them only occasionally—were careful to place the customary Italian terms next to them. Those, like Schumann, MacDowell, and Debussy, who wished for nationalistic reasons to use their own languages, translated the Italian terms instead of relying solely on the metronome. Bartók and Stravinsky, however, usually indicated the tempo by metronome marks alone. But they did so for structural, not instructional, reasons. They desired not so much a particular tempo as an unyielding beat during the course of the composition. To cap this desultory attitude toward the metronome, it is a fact that whether or not the composer offers performers metronome marks, no two of them play his music in exactly the same tempo.

6 THE PERFORMER AS COAUTHOR

The relation of the performer to the composer, therefore, is a very special one. It could not be otherwise where the score is a script, where the function of notation is to detail compositional processes, and where there is an oral supplement to the score in the form of a prevailing idiom. This special relation is none other than coauthorship. In the words of R. G. Collingwood, "Every performer is co-author of the work he performs. This is obvious enough, but in our tradition of the last hundred years and more, we have been constantly shutting our eyes to it."[15] We may add that the blindness has not been limited to the field of music. It has obscured the relation of the actors, scene designers, and other members of the stage to the playwright, the relation of the machinist to the designer, of the builder to the architect, and similar relations in many other areas.

A special relation calls for a special sense of responsibility. The very consciousness of coauthorship should make the performer doubly careful about any carelessness or insufficient study, for these are fatal to the composer's interests. The cultivation of this sense of responsibility must begin early. One way of convincing students of the danger in laxity is to test their knowledge of certain pertinent details about a composer. For example, How did Debussy look?; What sort of person was he?; What is the student's general impression of the man? Those who have never read his biography or seen his picture almost invariably describe Debussy as tall, thin, delicate looking—in short, the conventional portrait of the poet.

While this may seem a harmless little game, something like imagining the appearance of a radio announcer from the sound of his voice, it has much more significance. Actually, Debussy was a strong, masculine person, a short, stocky man with a large head and a heavy, black beard. He was not only not effeminate but blunt and uncompromising in character, and he had a sarcastic, razor-edged wit that he used freely on his contemporaries as well as his predecessors. What is most important about this contrast between the actual and an imagined Debussy is the light it sheds on the student who is about to study his music. Clearly, the student who remains uninformed about Debussy's personality is relying, in a vague and indiscriminate way, on what we have called *conversance with idiom.* As he plays the music over and over again, he applies what he has heard about Debussy, what he remembers from other performances, and stray bits of information he has picked up here and there. If Debussy's music emerges effeminate and conventionally poetic under his fingers, it is not because the music possesses these qualities but because the student expected to find them there.

Sending the student to a biography and to Debussy's own writings for exact information will give greater promise of a suitable interpretation. He will look for qualities in the music that are more in keeping with this composer's personality. That is, he is not told to find sarcasm and biting wit in the music; he is to discover qualities that may be reconciled with a sarcastic and witty attitude of mind. For example, when a student approaches the performance of Debussy's *La Fille aux cheveux de lin* (Preludes, Book I, No. 8), he must divest himself of beliefs based on hearsay. The French attitude toward the senses is by no means effeminate or precious, and Debussy, who epitomized French qualities of mind, could be expected to have a more cogent objective than to paint a blonde-haired girl in tone. The clue is the title. The title comes from a poem by Leconte de Lisle which, in turn, is a translation of Robert Burns's "The Lassie with the Lint-white Locks." The first stanza of Burns's poem is as follows:

> Lassie wi' the lint-white locks,
> Bonnie lassie, artless lassie,
> Wilt thou wi' me tent the flocks,
> Wilt thou be my dearie O?

Of course, Debussy was aware that this poem is a love poem. But he was mainly interested in its folk aspect—more specifically, in the roots of Burns's poetry in folksong. Scottish folksong, like the music of China and Negro spirituals, uses the pentatonic or five-note scale. This scale is of more ancient origin than the seven-note major scale which has half-steps or leading-tones where the pentatonic has intervals of a third. Fig. 2 compares typical motives from Scottish folksong with those used by Debussy in the Prelude. Quite probably, Debussy's

FIG. 2
Motifs from Scottish folksong

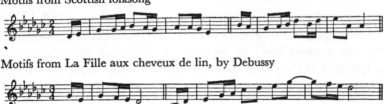

Motifs from La Fille aux cheveux de lin, by Debussy

interest in such less familiar scales was motivated by their greater suitability to his characteristic shifting harmonies and modal coloring.

7 FINDING THE CENTRAL PURPOSE

Every musical composition, whether or not its title is as helpful as Debussy's, has a *central purpose* in expression to which all of its elements contribute. A familiar way of stating the same thing is to say that the composer strives for variety within unity. Often, too, we speak of "the subject" of a piece of music. It is essential for the performer to be convinced that he has discovered this central purpose or subject. Otherwise, his rendition, however skillful or even tasteful it is, will be fragmentary and jarring, will not reconcile all the elements of the musical score. As we shall later explain in greater detail, *appropriateness* is the cardinal virtue of interpretation. The student who starts out with Scotland and the contours of Scottish folksong rather than the blonde-haired girl as the subject of Debussy's prelude will have a better chance of achieving this appropriateness in interpretation.

Occasionally, Brahms also added a subtitle or a few lines of poetry to his usually generic titles. For example, he placed the following fragment from Herder's collection of Scottish folk-poetry at the heading of his Intermezzo in E flat major, Op. 117, No. 1:

> Sleep, sleep, my child, sleep safe and sound
> It grieves me sorely to see thee weep.

His central purpose, therefore, was to compose a lullaby or cradlesong. The discovery of this subject is of great importance, but the student must go further. He will find that the locale is British folksong and that the singer is the deserted wife of a sailor. Fig. 3(a) compares the melody of the Intermezzo with

FIG. 3

(a) English folksong, Pretty Polly Oliver

Theme of Intermezzo in E-flat major, Op. 117, No. 1, by Brahms

(b) Middle section of Intermezzo

the well-known British folksong *Pretty Polly Oliver*. This folksong, though different in subject matter, is of a type that might have suggested to Brahms certain features of his theme. As to the enigmatic section in E-flat minor, (b), the intention to write a cradlesong solves the problem: The bass, as in Schumann's *Wiegenliedchen*, Op. 124, No. 6, and Chopin's Berceuse, creates a rocking effect. It will be essential in the performance not to hold the damper pedal during the rests in the bass.

When the composer does not affix a title or a poem to his music, the search extends to his letters or to contemporary references. The object is not to find a "program" or implied libretto for the music but to discover clues to its central purpose. At the heading of his Piano Sonata No. 14 in C-sharp minor, Op. 27, No. 2, Beethoven has placed only *Quasi una fantasia*, an indication that he was taking a freer attitude and departing from the usual requirements for the first movement of a sonata. A hearsay interpretation based on the appellation *Moonlight Sonata* is of course silly. Alexander Wheelock Thayer, in his definitive biography of Beethoven, refers to a contemporary letter linking the Sonata with the German poet Seume's

Fig. 4

(a) Harmonic progression of first theme, Adagio sostenuto, Piano Sonata No. 14 in C-sharp minor, Op. 27, No. 2, by Beethoven

(b) Harmonic progression of chorale, Gott hat das Evangelium, by Bach

Die Beterin (*The Young Girl at Prayer*).[16] This clue, with its connotation of religious feeling, is much more useful. But the starting point for organizing the elements in the first movement of the Sonata into a pattern of appropriateness is the practice of composing chorale preludes to Lutheran hymn tunes. Fig. 4(a), the harmonic progression of Beethoven's theme, and (b), Bach's harmonies for a closely similar chorale melody, show that Beethoven modeled the music on the progressions and strong cadences of the chorale idiom, selecting the particularly expressive type that places the tonic harmony on the upbeat and the dominant on the downbeat. Beethoven has "modernized" the usually contrapuntal middle voice into simple, repetitive triplets, but, in general, the movement belongs in the same category as Bach's chorale prelude *Ich ruf' zu dir*.

In the case of other first movements of Beethoven's piano sonatas, which can be listed on programs only by their tempi,

FIG. 5

First movement, Themes I and II, Piano Sonata No. 1 in F minor, Op. 2, No. 1, by Beethoven

FIG. 6

(a) First movement, Theme 1, Piano Sonata No. 10 in G major, Op. 14, No. 2, by Beethoven

(b) Same movement, Theme II   (c)

as, for example, *Allegro moderato*, *Allegro con brio*, etc., the clues to the factors making for appropriateness lie in the relation between the first and second themes. In the Sonata No. 1 in F minor, Op. 2, No. 1, Fig. 5, the relation is that of an inversion that emphasizes their dynamic, driving force and confirms the need for and location of the sforzandi. In the Sonata No. 10 in G major, Op. 14, No. 2, the relation is more subtle and not

FIG. 7
First movement, Piano Sonata in G major, K.283, by Mozart

(e)   Development Section

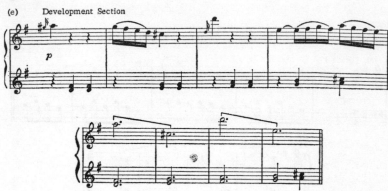

at once apparent. However, the structural basis of the first theme is Fig. 6(a). That of the second theme is (b). Consequently, the relation between the two themes is that of sequential thirds within an octave, (c). The performer, then, would do well to give special significance to the broken octave.

The themes and sections in Mozart's sonatas are related in the same subtle way. To the casual listener, they often seem too light-hearted, too freely associated, to combine toward one central purpose. While it is not up to the performer to show how wrong this judgment is, the interpretation of Mozart's music requires his greatest abilities and should never be assigned to elementary students. For example, in the opening bars of the Piano Sonata in G major, K.283, the performer must view the theme, Fig. 7(a), not so much in terms of its minuet rhythm as in terms of its outline, (b). In this way, the apparently diverse materials of the second theme, (c), the closing theme, (d), and the development, (e), all contribute to the same central purpose, which has to do with the effect of two descending intervals, a sixth and a seventh.

Where movements in three-part rather than sonata form are concerned, the relation between the materials of the two different sections is apt to seem even more remote and not to contribute to one main subject. This lack of connection is often cited in the case of Schubert's music, and Schubert is accused of rambling despite the evident beauties of his themes. However, his central purpose is always discoverable, and suitable performance can bring it out. For example, the opening theme of his Impromptu in E-flat major, Op. 90, No. 2, Fig. 8(a), seems at first to be unrelated to the main theme of the middle section, (b). It is true that the melodic contours are not similar, but the underlying rhythm is the same, (c). Consequently, the performer who would give unity to this Impromptu and demonstrate the appropriateness of all its elements must give due emphasis to the rhythm of the bass, the brackets in (a), as opposed to the triplets in the treble, and also to the rhythm of the harmonic progression which is in dotted half notes (minims). In other words, the player performs in such a way that by the time the middle section arrives, a gradually increasing rhythmic emphasis and turbulence will cause the listener to

FIG. 8

(a) Measures 1–4, Impromptu in E-flat major, Op. 90, No. 2, by Schubert

(b) Middle section of Impromptu

(c) Basic rhythms of first section

Basic rhythms of middle section

(d) Measure 34

accept its vitality as completely appropriate. Measure 34, (d), becomes especially significant to this purpose.

These examples are sufficient at this point to explain the significance of discovering the central purpose of a composition. The performer becomes convinced that he has found the clue to making all the elements in it appropriate to one another, and his performance is successful when his auditors become similarly convinced. He and they feel that his interpretation is *justified*. The composer has been influenced by many different associations of thought in arriving at the content of his music. If the composition is well written, the notation symbols will offer clues to the content and also to the nature of the associations that prompted it. In view of the oral supplement to the score, the validation of these clues is easier when the composer has supplied an other than generic title or quoted lines from a poem, or, if he has not done so, when contemporary references offer supporting evidence.

I say that the validation is "easier," not necessarily easy. Because the performer must be prepared to hear other interpretations, even from the same set of facts about the score's central purpose, he can only become convinced and never absolutely certain that his interpretation is valid. The oral supplement, the multiple significance of notation symbols, the possibility of an infinite number of renditions—these factors make the score merely the top of a mountain that lies mainly below the surface, and they explain why the performer's sense of having made the right decisions must be deeply rooted in his unconscious mind and his early childhood.

It is in this initial period that some children, due to innate sensitivity and also to home environment, acquire a large musical vocabulary and become familiar with musical phraseology much earlier than others. Then later on, when they encounter the notation symbols, they have a readiness that enables them to match these symbols with the vocabulary and phraseology they already know. To a highly significant extent they divine or apprehend the music rather than "read" it. Such an approach is ideally suited to the infinite nature of the score, and it should be consciously cultivated by the later comers to music study who have not had the benefit of the early conversance with idiom. It insures as well against mistaking the score for a series of instructions to the performer.

In discovering the central purpose of a composition, therefore, the basic question is not whether the use of factual evidence obviates the need for musical intuition but whether the use of musical intuition obviates the need for factual evidence. The best answer to this question that I know was given by the 19th-century physicist John Tyndall, in an anecdote about Michael Faraday, the famous scientist in the field of electricity. Tyndall was about to show Faraday an experiment he had been working on when Faraday tapped him on the shoulder and asked, "What am I to look for?" Precisely because Faraday was such a capable observer, he might have taken in innumerable nonrelevant details unless forewarned where to focus his attention. Similarly, no matter how highly developed a performer's intuition may be, he needs guidance where to apply it. Were this not so, we would not encounter instances when the same performer delights us with one composer and disappoints us with another. Perhaps the most common among these is successful performance of Chopin or Debussy and not of J. S. Bach. Yet Harold Samuel was a singular case of the reverse. He was acclaimed for his all-Bach programs, but he could not induce audiences to flock to his varied programs.

The performer's need to assist his intuitive powers reminds us of a similar situation facing the composer. In flashes of insight, the composer discovers musical themes. But these themes come at the very beginning of his work and he must extend them into long, complete compositions. We say that the music is "padded" when there are stretches of arid passagework between attractive themes. To avoid patchiness, the composer studies arduously, delves deeply into his subject, compares it with other works, strives for a unity of purpose. Then his music seems one flash of intuition from beginning to end, but the erasures in his manuscript tell the true story. In the same way, the performer may be able to make certain passages vivid through intuitive insight and yet leave other sections—perhaps the very same developments and episodes where the composer had to keep his inspiration from flagging—dry, lifeless, superficially glittering. He, too, must learn to ignite the whole composition with the sparks from isolated phrases. Toward this end, he can find no better aid than that research into the personality of the composer and into the circumstances surrounding production of the music which uncovers significant details and fuses them into one central purpose.

II PERFORMANCE AS THE SYNTHESIS OF THE CATEGORIES OF METHOD

8 THE MEANING OF PRACTICING

One may not at first see why a chapter on the study and teaching of performance belongs here rather than only in books or manuals on how to play instruments. In the context of the points we have made, however, an expression like "to play the piano" has very little meaning beyond absent-minded strumming. We have translated it into "to perform a musical score for piano" and have defined each of these terms. By "musical score" is meant the framework for an infinite number of performances. There are as many different interpretations of the score as there are players who perform it. Each of these interpretations is therefore a joint effort of the performer and the composer, a true example of coauthorship. The performer qualifies as a coauthor by discovering the central purpose of the score. That is, he finds the characteristics in a composition that in his opinion make its elements appropriate to one another; he calls upon one of three categories of method, knowledge of musical *context*. Also, he understands how those elements contribute to one total musical structure; this is a second category of method, training in structural *analysis*.

By "performing," the player endeavors to confirm his status as coauthor. The composer may perform his own music, like the author of a play who acts in it, but his interpretation still remains only one out of the infinite number of possibilities.

In either case, "performance" means to communicate discovery of the central purpose of the score to the listener. Consequently, the term "for piano" signifies that the composer has planned for the use of this instrument in communicating with the listener. A pianist is to employ the resources of the piano to make the listener aware of the appropriateness among all the elements of the composition. Here, only as one part of the process, the performer requisitions a third category, *muscular* control over the instrument.

From this explanation of what "playing the piano" means, it follows that once a pianist declares his intention of performing a musical score, he cannot so much as touch the keyboard for this purpose without interpreting. Every rendition is a performance whether the player is reading the score for the first time or is practicing or has reached a final interpretation. The performance may be bad or good at any of these stages, and in the earlier ones there may be elements that are worth retaining in the later. For these reasons, a player is simply deluding himself if he thinks that reading and practicing the score are merely preparatory to a later stage when interpretation begins. Each time and in any way that the player addresses himself to the score, he has taken a step toward a completed rendition. How he handles such steps is therefore of the utmost importance.

Good teaching has recognized this fact by striving to prevent practicing from degenerating into mechanical exercise. An immense number of methods have been devised, among them the composition of etudes. An etude or study tries to remain good music while it emphasizes one muscular task. Here, the names of Clementi, who influenced Beethoven's piano figuration, and Czerny, teacher of Liszt, come most readily to mind. However, almost every composer in a long list from Couperin and Bach to Debussy tried his hand at writing etudes. The value of a method, then, is judged by how well it serves the standards of good music, by how well it maintains the conditions of performance.

To maintain the conditions of performance, to have the student study performance and not merely study for performance, is a difficult objective. Each of the innumerable methods fails to achieve it in some respect, chiefly because no method can claim to be the best or the only one. The study of performance is so complex that to extol the virtues of one approach is to blind oneself to the necessity of another. Clearly, the solution is not to select one method but to extract values from them all by synthesizing the three categories to which they belong. To be successful, teaching must devote attention to all three of the basic aspects of study, the muscular, the contextual, and the analytic. And all three must be kept constantly in view and interconnected. The purpose of muscular organization is to express the significance or context of the music as revealed by analysis of its structure.

Our intention in this chapter, then, is to describe the process of achieving performance of the score on an instrument as the synthesis of the three categories of method. Using the methods of teaching the pianist as a model, we shall follow him from the moment he places the score on the stand to his final rendition. In the face of the profusion of methods, we shall adopt the plan of discussing those of the three teachers who are most often associated with each category, Tobias Matthay, Alfred Cortot, and Heinrich Schenker.[17] It should be understood that their teachings were in part anticipated by other teachers and have been amplified by still others since. Indeed, other methods may be substituted for these provided that they illustrate the categories. For our objective is to synthesize not the methods themselves but the categories into which they all fall. When our purpose has been fulfilled, we shall have a way of performing music, not merely a way of learning to perform music. We will have shown that practicing, like rehearsing, is simply not yet completely realized performance.

9 MATTHAY AND MUSCULAR TRAINING

Tobias Matthay (1858–1945), after a long association with the Royal Academy of Music both as student and teacher, founded his own school for the dissemination of his ideas on teaching. His *Act of Touch* (1903) was the first definitive statement of his views and it formed the kernel for his later books on teaching and interpretation. He had observed that students who seemed to be hampered by poor muscular endowment were in reality choosing the wrong muscular motions, and he set out to help them realize that some motions are more suited to carry out a given task than others.

Matthay drew the students' attention to the mechanism of the piano because muscular adjustment must be made in terms of the instrument. For example, he emphasized the fact that the piano hammer has struck the string and rebounded before the key-lever reaches the key-bed, or felt pad, that stops its motion. He thereby established the superiority of producing tone through motion over production by a blow. The student was counseled to "listen for the beginning of sound," and since this moment is identical with neither the contact of the finger and key-surface nor the contact of key-lever and key-bed, he was warned against "knocking the key-lever by concussion against its surface" and against "squeezing the key upon its bed." To knock against the key-surface or key-bed is to delude oneself about the moment of tone production and misuse the instrument's mechanism. Tone is produced through the motion of the key-lever at an intangible moment in its arc. By directing the student's attention to this fact, Matthay placed him on the right road, so that thereafter he developed muscular control without losing sight of the factor of motion in tone production.[18]

Emphasis on motion as opposed to impact means greater freedom in playing. The arm and wrist can be brought into play in addition to finger action. Matthay was then able to distinguish among three main types of touch and to assign them to different roles in playing. "The distinction between Finger-touch, Hand-touch, and Arm-touch depends upon which one of the three muscular components is slightly in excess of the other two, during the process of key-descent." This continual conjunction of large and small motions suggests that "the preliminary fall of the limb upon the key-surface arise from Relaxation," which is defined as "the ease derived from the omission of all unnecessary physical exertion." As the player compares the various tonal effects that may be secured with the aid of a relaxed swing, he learns to analyze motion according to "the isolation of each set of muscular impulses from its opposite set." He senses "the added impetus (energy momentarily applied to the key during descent)," a force which takes an upward instead of the expected downward direction due to the flexibility of the wrist joint as it feels an "upward reaction from the key against knuckle and wrist."

As this description shows, Matthay's organization of muscular energy offers a proper counterpart to the detail of the musical score. The forces in notation are matched by the forces in muscular motion. Yet, as we have said, no one method can stand alone, particularly when its major contribution is to only one of the three categories we have defined. In his subsequent books, Matthay was forced to deal with the other two categories, interpretation and analysis, but as he had dealt with them only in passing or during actual lessons, he was not prepared to systematize them to the same extent as his organization of muscular training. For example, Matthay does caution against treating the musical passage as "dead, disconnected blocks or chunks," a tendency that sets in when attention is unduly centered on single notes for muscular purposes. But he proposed to remedy this condition by a rather weak arrow system that pointed ahead to the state of rest afforded by cadences at the end of phrases. A "rhythmic principle," a "sense of progressing somewhere," offered the stress that meanwhile moved the music forward to the cadence. By apportioning touch in terms of such stress and rest, the stagnation resulting from planned acts of touch would be overcome. As we read this type of advice, we cannot help contrasting it with the thoroughness of Matthay's treatment of muscular motion.

Furthermore, Matthay was forced to answer those who criticized his method for setting up a mechanical ideal on one side and an interpretive ideal on the other, without a perceptible bridge between them. Perhaps his followers were more responsible than he for this criticism. Matthay had indeed emphasized the right motion for the right purpose, but some of his disciples began to act as if the muscles had interpretive powers. Matthay thereupon defended his position: "In giving the necessarily close attention to the wherewithal of Expression, there is always this great danger lurking in us, that we are liable not only to forget Art in the doing of it, but liable to forget what should be the purpose of Art—the very purpose of our pursuit." He was separating the act of touch from the imagined tone only for purposes of discussion. When it came to the actuality of teaching, touch and tone were united through an intermediary, a form of "musical attention or listening" that had the power of "unconsciously guiding the artist (or student) to choose the exact combination of colors and shapes that will render his conception—facts of the imagination—into physical actuality." [19]

Here, we again come upon the inevitable results of systematizing one category and not the other two. The remaining categories are left in a vague state where some form of musical talent is to come to the student's aid. It is important to note that some methods maintain that the muscles will take care of themselves if the student knows how to analyze the music properly. Matthay, in opposing this view and in not depending upon a natural flair for muscular dexterity, had in effect done the same thing to context and analysis that such other methods did to the muscular. He had placed them in the realm of "unconscious guidance" where they depend upon an indefinite form of talent. Perhaps one person has more talent than the next, but until we have systematized all three categories, we have not located the point where we have done all we can to equip the student.

Matthay also had to answer his critics about the teacher's role. As the muscular advice became more and more detailed, it was increasingly necessary to discriminate between the teacher's analysis of the touch–tone relation and the student's mastery of it. Naturally, in order to suggest steps to the student, the teacher has to analyze his own accomplishment. Without some guarantees in advance that both student and teacher have the same "facts of the imagination" in mind, these steps can easily become ends instead of means. Should this happen, the zeal of the teacher and the student's ambition lavish attention upon one note at a time, as if the total effect of a passage could be secured in this way. Then both teacher and student are guilty of mistaking clarity of execution for clarity of expression. A muscular rendition ensues, dominated by convenience and facility. Accordingly, Matthay had to remind the teacher that unless he patiently waits until the student has formed interpretive ideas, it will be "difficult to draw the line between merely *conducting* a performance of the teacher through the pupil's fingers and correctly teaching him by prompting him to play on his own initiative." [20]

We can easily recall performances that bear out the necessity for this admonition. First, there are the renditions of child performers. Rightfully, a prodigy should show flashes of talent amid exaggerations, roughnesses, and naive musical ideas. If, instead, the child plays with the polish and dexterity of a seasoned performer, we may be sure that the teacher has merely "conducted a performance through the pupil's fingers." Such playing is indeed a tribute to the teacher's power of self-analysis and the pupil's aptitude, but it also explains why prodigies often fail to fulfill their promise. Secondly, there are the renditions that, as we said in the preceding chapter, treat the score as a statement of performance values. Relieved of solving the thorny problems of the context, the player feels free to accommodate his muscles to standard demands. Actually, he is no more skillful than the performer who takes context into account, but he sounds that way. Submission to the context effaces the performer, places a screen between him and the audience, and without it, the skill factor becomes obvious. Eventually, however, failure to subordinate muscular skill to the context catches up with the player and he hears that his performances "show more technique than expression."

In our synthesis of methods, muscular organization must be given a highly important place, and the form it should take must be much as Matthay conceived it. But his less successful efforts to integrate it with context and analysis bring out all the more that, even if another type of muscular organization than Matthay's is preferred, it can occupy only one share of the total method. Due to the fluidity of music and the limits upon conscious analysis, planning acts of touch is possible only up to a point. Such planning is restricted to affording information about the muscles and the instrument, to revealing the availability of touch, not its immediate application. For the stimulus in musical performance, one must go to the score, to relationships among groups of tones. To make muscular possibilities into a reality called "technique" is like trying to make a suit of clothes stand by itself.

Muscular interconnections do not have an independent status. They owe their existence only to the interconnections in music itself. It is true that music is repetitive from composer to composer, that different compositions use similar patterns, note values, and processes, and the muscular motions that these evoke may be codified much as musical materials are codified. But widespread use of muscular motions is not an adequate reason for giving them objective reality. They compare with one another, never become identical. Should a player discover an especially convenient way of handling a frequently appearing group of tones, such as a scale, he could not thereafter use it every time a scale occurred. For then he would be assuming that a scale always had the same contextual significance, which is certainly not the case, and if he behaved likewise toward other common groups of tones, his playing would eventually become uniform for all composers and compositions. The stimulus for performance would no longer be in the score but in his own muscular organization. It could then be said with justice that he possessed a technique. However, this possession would not save his performance from being inadequate.

10   CORTOT AND POETIC DESCRIPTION

Alfred Cortot (1877–1963) began his career as a virtuoso pianist almost immediately after graduating, *première prix,* from the Paris Conservatoire. Yet he devoted a considerable amount of time to teaching, first as professor at the Conservatoire and later at the École Normale de Musique. The fruits of this teaching were his *éditions de travail* of Chopin, Liszt, and Schumann and his systematic method called *Rational Principles of Piano Technique* (1928). Although he was a pianist of formidable powers, the main emphasis in these pedagogic works is on poetic description of music, what we have called "the context." Thus, in contrast to Matthay, they contain few detailed analyses of touch and few references to the instrument's mechanism, but they fairly glow with poetic imagery. The following quotation is typical:

> The impassioned élan and quickened ardor which characterize the first *Prelude* of Chopin are achieved through a clear articulation of its syncopated figure which, from measure to measure, leads the melodic line ever upward, breathless and feverish, until it reaches a climax of exaltation in measures 21 to 24, the culminating point of an arc which then undergoes a short diminuendo, during which the sonority of the tone lessens, without affecting the insistent character of the dominant rhythmic pattern, which may be likened to the palpitations of a heart overcome by emotion.[21]

In this long single sentence, one can almost picture a performance of the Prelude, itself one uninterrupted statement from beginning to end.

We might at first attribute the contrast with Matthay to the volatile temperament of the French as compared with the reticence of the English. The difference, however, goes much deeper and is actually in the steps of the methods themselves. Before beginning the study of a new composition, Cortot insisted that the student prepare a detailed commentary on its origin, replete with facts, dates, relevant biography, and quotations from the letters of the composer and his contemporaries. He also required of the student a description of the music, full of imagery and poetic insights and recording the effect it had had on his own sensibility. The commentary and description are there not as a whim of fancy but as a closely reasoned part of the method. They are the insurance that the imaginative context will take precedence over the work with the muscles and that the student will have definite ideas about an interpretation before starting to play.

Next, Cortot's method defines the type of muscular difficulty and breaks up that difficulty into small components: "The essential rule of this method is to practice, not the difficult passage, but the difficulty contained in it, by starting such practice from its very root." [22] This distinction between "the difficult passage" and "the difficulty contained in it" leads to the construction of exercises made from some portion of the passage or from a revision of its tones. The difficulty of the passage is conceived as compound, as the end result of a number of component difficulties, each of which requires its own, different adjustment from the muscles. For example, Cortot designs the following four exercises[23] in terms of four components that he has perceived within the total difficulty:

FIG. 9

Measures 9-10, Presto finale, Ballade in G minor, Op. 23, by Chopin

Exercises

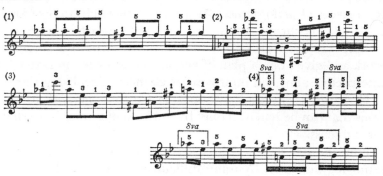

These exercises apply to measures 9 and 10 of the concluding *Presto* in Chopin's Ballade in G minor, Op. 23. Exercise (1) is for the mutual substitution of thumb and 5th finger; (2) for the exchange of broken octaves; (3) for the connection between the intermediate fingers and the thumb; (4) for the position and alternation of the intermediate fingers and the 5th finger. The total difficulty is defined as a demand upon the suppleness of movements of the wrist.

The essence of Cortot's approach, then, is two-pronged: It is contained in a constant relationship between the poetic image to be achieved and the muscular difficulty to be overcome. As the student works on the exercises, Cortot continually urges him to keep the context in mind: "There must be complete obedience of the muscles to the imagination. . . . This means long and detailed work, but it is the work of a true musician. And, as Schumann said, only the insensitive pianist will take no pleasure in doing it." [24] The great advantage of this approach is that it thrusts concern with the context into the midst of concern with the muscles. When the student arrives at the scales near the end of the Ballade, they must be "trenchant," "imperious," and he must work "not simply for the sole purpose of being correct" but "to insure their éclat and plasticity."

There are other advantages to Cortot's approach as well. The student deals with specific passages rather than with piano playing as a whole. The exercises create conditions that bring about the requisite muscular motions and that anticipate the final stages of performance. As a result, they help to overcome the characteristically distasteful aspect of the earlier stages, the atmosphere of drudgery. Cortot has reached into the student's work and given him a plan of action that at once motivates his interpretive aims and improves his chances of realizing them.

However, there are limitations to Cortot's method, limitations that can be removed only by the kind of synthesis we shall later discuss.

First, he has designed his exercises for the sole purpose of removing difficulty. By using difficulty as the basis, he fails to define clearly the status of the student who is to employ the exercises. It is as if he were asking himself, from a position of mastery, what *his* performance of the composition would require. Side by side, then, with the poetic descriptions that only a highly advanced muscular control could apply, he places basic exercises for passage of the thumb, or for control of the black keys, or for polyphonic playing. Such exercises are didactic rather than gauged to the type of student who could be expected to be playing the composition. They represent a *reculer pour mieux sauter*, a strategic retreat, and the student is left to puzzle how extensive a retreat to make, how far back to begin the steps toward the final rendition.

Conceivably, a student who felt that he already had control over the passage of the thumb, over the black keys, over polyphonic playing, could skip the exercises and begin at once to apply the context. But if he omitted the exercise, he would place his achievement of the context in jeopardy because each one of them has some bearing on its elements. If the exercises are not done, the particular value of the method, an intertwining of context with skill, will be lost. This circumstance shows that Cortot did not regard his approach as performance itself but rather as preparation for performance. He, too, visualized a realm beyond the student's work where an indefinite talent is to operate: "But although the interpreter's attention should be engrossed by the search for this tone-coloring, its successful achievement rests ultimately upon questions of personal emotion and individual sensibility, questions which stand far above a dry aesthetic analysis and far above pedagogic indication." [25] Again, before such reliance on talent, we must ask whether a method has done for the student all it can.

Second, Cortot did not deal with the questions surrounding the idea of "tone painting," that is, those questions that arise whenever we relate the world of music to the actual world. When he describes a passage poetically, he confidently expects everyone to agree with him, and while we are struck by and take pleasure in the aptness of his characterization, we must be prepared to admit that someone else might find a somewhat different poetic content in the music he describes. We must not forget, too, that some people adamantly deny any connection between the actual and the musical worlds. These are real problems, and the right to include the contextual category in a method depends upon solving them. Unless it shows how experience of the actual world is reflected in music and reflected in a way that permits varied interpretation, a contextual method builds a house of cards that will collapse at the first breath of skepticism.

Finally, Cortot's method, like that of Matthay, does not include those elements that are grouped under the heading of structural analysis and that are obviously needed in performance. Perhaps both Cortot and Matthay assumed that the student would also be taking courses in harmonic analysis, counterpoint, and form. In any case, such training plays no direct role either in Matthay's planning of the act of touch or in Cortot's overcoming of muscular difficulty. Yet no method can afford to take understanding of musical structure for granted. If it does so, it risks certain anomalies in student progress. Some students study harmony and never apply this knowledge to performance; others can play a piece but not sketch it; still others reach the point of memorizing a piece but cannot play the theme apart from its setting. Above all, only when the method requisitions the musical understanding at every step in rendition will it banish that perennial bogey, the difference between the "theoretical" and the "applied."

11 SCHENKER AND HARMONIC ANALYSIS

Heinrich Schenker (1868–1935) studied at the Vienna Conservatory with Bruckner, and his first compositions had the distinction of being recommended for publication by Brahms. But he soon left the field of composition to devote himself completely to musical theory and research. The essence of his teachings is contained in his *New Musical Theories and Fantasies*, the three volumes of which appeared over the period 1906–35. Unlike Matthay and Cortot, Schenker did not limit his system to the purposes of performance. But he intended it to be applied to performance: "The performance of a musical art-work can be based only on an organically-evolved coherence." [26]

The easiest, if not entirely accurate, way to describe Schenker's attitude toward musical structure is to compare it with the composer's point of view in writing a theme and variations. While each variation makes sense, it owes its structure to the plan behind the theme. In a similar fashion, Schenker finds a basic plan that influenced the structure of a composition, as if the composer had written a variation without stating the theme. He views music in three guises: the *background* (in our comparison, the theme), the *middleground* (some of the simpler variations), and the *foreground* (the most complex variation). The background is a basic pattern that is transformed into the foreground or final form of the composition by the activity of the middleground. Since the composer presents only the foreground, it is the function of analysis to penetrate to the middle and background. Musical analysis, then, is defined as an effort to discover the basic pattern of the background from the foreground by using reduction techniques offered by the middleground.

In Schenker's approach, this effort of analysis is largely harmonic. With the aid of tonality, he reduces the melodic aspects of the foreground to a prime line within the compass of an octave, and by treating some chords as subordinate to others, he finds a minimum pattern for the bass as well. Thus reduced, musical structure ultimately becomes equivalent to playing the notes of the tonic chord in downward succession from one octave to the next while the same notes in the reverse or upward succession are being played in the bass. Such upward and downward breakage of the tonic chord provides the framework for the varieties in musical presentation, in much the same manner that steel girders support the stonework of a building. In reaching this ultimate simplicity, Schenker found two factors troublesome. He had to limit the subdominant to use as a neighboring chord and to require that all subsidiary modulation (or passing reference to related keys) take place within an octave of its starting point.

The idea of reducing a passage to simpler terms is the keystone of all types of musical analysis. It is comparable to the method of diagramming sentences that uses oblique lines to connect adjectives, adverbs, and clauses on a lower line to the subject noun and the predicate verb on a line above. The chief difference between Schenker's analysis and other types, therefore, does not lie in the idea of reduction. Since the simultaneous upward and downward breakage of the tonic chord that is the ultimate background also constitutes a cadence, the difference lies in his use of the cadence in a new sense—as applying in a large, comprehensive way to the entire course of a composition. Previously, the term "cadence" was limited to constructions at the end of the musical phrase that provide sensations of relative conclusiveness, as punctuation does for sentences. As Schenker views the cadence, it can take place over several hundred measures, and its pivotal points can be located far apart in different large sections of the total form.

This view lends the strong, directional force of the cadence to the unfolding of an entire composition. A feeling of unity is derived from the forces of stress and resolution that are contained within the powerful dominant–tonic relationship. Thus, Schenker enlarged the concept of tonally related sections by giving dynamic import to the background pattern itself. The basic cadence had a structure of its own that persisted throughout the composition despite the varied structures of the foreground presentation. We can now see why the comparison of Schenker's method with the concept of theme and variations is only partly accurate. His method is that of a pyramid balanced on its point, whereas the concept of theme and variations is that of a building resting squarely on its foundation. Nevertheless, the *instrument* that makes Schenker's method possible is the *technique of variation* of which the theme and variations is the most representative instance.

That Schenker's ideas belong in a synthesis of methods is unquestioned. They contribute to the third area, the area of musical understanding, and they help to fulfill its needs in a valuable way. We can see how Schenker's basic plan for a composition would enable a student to memorize more easily and to reduce overdependence on repetition. It promotes the ability to sketch, and trying the passage in reduced forms has the effect of clarifying the features of the final form. Above all, it endows the student with the powers inherent in a synopsis or in a panoramic view, so that he can perceive more clearly what each section contributes to the whole. His performance emerges better proportioned. One section seems to demand the next rather than merely precede it, and the student learns to allot his energies more suitably, with the result that climaxes are properly placed and achieved with a sense of fitness.

Yet valuable as Schenker's teachings are, they do not, for several reasons, entirely meet the requirements of the third or analytic area of a synthesized method. First, the concept of one gigantic cadence forced Schenker to assert the supremacy of the dominant–tonic relationship among the forces that lend unity to a composition. He had then to lean heavily on the epoch when that relationship reached its climax—his list of examples begins mainly with Bach and stops short of Wagner and Debussy. Recently, Felix Salzer, in his book *Structural Hearing*, has extended this list in both directions.[27] He claims that Schenker's theories apply beyond the dominant–tonic relationship and supports this claim by making a distinction between "chord grammar"—that is, the origin of chords in scales and keys—and "chord significance," the ways to use them for musical purposes. Whatever the scope of Schenker may be, Salzer's ideas are useful as a plea to retain the significance of the tonic, in view of the dilemma posed by the twelve-note system, and incidentally as a plan for the sequence of courses in music study.

Second, Schenker's emphasis on harmony as the main tool of analysis curtails the importance of rhythm and melody. It seems more logical to treat harmony as one among a variety of means at the disposal of the composer, a powerful one, to be sure, but one that he uses to varying extents from composition to composition. Indeed, rhythm and melody sometimes outweigh harmony in significance for the structure. In this sense, a healthy musical art does not depend upon tonal matters per se. It depends upon keeping their contribution to the total purpose of a composition in proportion.

Third, Schenker's approach tends to reduce the importance of the element he called the foreground. From his synoptic analyses, one can mistakenly conclude that the background contains most of the meaning of music. The term *prolongation* is critical in this respect. Schenker uses it in the sense that the foreground ramifies or implements the processes already contained in the background. The implication is that the foreground would not hang together were there not connections already existing in the background. However, if a composer takes eight measures instead of four to progress from the tonic to the dominant—that is, "prolongs" the background to the extent of eight measures instead of four—this fact is as important to the meaning of the music as the locations of the tonic and dominant are.

The significance of the background, then, is as dependent upon the foreground as the latter is on the former. The progression from tonic to dominant has no existence in itself, except in a book on harmony, and it does not become a reality because it required four measures in one piece and eight in another. Each time that music is composed, the background must be achieved in terms of the foreground in just as strong a sense as the foreground is achieved in terms of the background. We must stop short, therefore, of giving the background meaning in itself. Otherwise, we end with raw materials or abstract potential that have enormous possibilities only because nothing has as yet been done with them.

There is a sort of satisfaction in reducing a composition to a minimum of notes. Then one can say it is all so simple: "all the composer had to do was . . ." The self-deception is obvious. It mistakes the possibilities of musical materials for the possibilities of expression, and we have only to try our hand at expression to find out the difference. The value of reduction to the "lower terms" of fewer notes is the light it can shed on the foreground, and yet, as we shall soon explain, it can do so only under further conditions. We must still know what to look for when we return to the foreground from analyzing the background. If we merely try to generalize about the practices of an epoch or to discover similar procedures among composers of different centuries, we will observe music instead of experiencing it. Each composition is an individual entity and the work of one particular man, and unless we derive its meaning primarily from the foreground, it will lose its identity as part of life in the past and become an incident in an evolution or a trend.

12 LAYER ANALYSIS

The time has come to attempt a synthesis of the muscular, contextual, and analytic categories in method and to integrate the diverse contributions of Matthay, Cortot, and Schenker. The means to do so is at hand in a centrally important factor that we shall call *layer analysis*. The first step is to change the basis for the exercises that bring about performance of the passage. As we have seen, Cortot based his exercises on the muscular difficulty of the passage. Instead, the synthesized method conceives its exercises as steps in understanding the passage's structure. This new basis for the creation of exercises is layer analysis. The following exercises are for the same two measures that Cortot analyzed on the basis of muscular difficulty (Fig. 9 in Section 10), and comparison with Cortot's exercises will reveal the difference in approach:

FIG. 10
Exercises

Fig. 10(a) presents the first stage in understanding the passage. This exercise reveals that the passage depends upon the effect of the Neapolitan sixth-chord (a chord obtained by lowering the second degree of the minor scale) and is therefore related to the Ballade's opening bars, which utilize the same chord. Exercises (b) and (c) illustrate the change in pianistic style from late 18th-century to early 19th-century idiom, a change to which Chopin made important contributions. They enable the student to contrast Chopin's distribution of tones with that of his predecessors and, already at this point, to form an idea of the scale of dynamics that the performance will require.

Exercise (d) involves the use of the term *asynchronization*. We shall borrow this term from psychology, although it has a more limited meaning there, and use it extensively later on. Asynchronization, as we are using the term, has the same significance as breaking or arpeggiating a chord but is not limited to presenting the chordal notes in the order of rising or descending pitch. That is, besides the orders 1—3—5—8 and 8—5—3—1, it includes such other possibilities as 1—5—3—8, 8—3—5—1, 3—5—8—1, as well as permutations in which two or even three out of the four constituent tones are sounded together. Exercise (d), then, shows that the composer has asynchronized the harmonies and raised the scale of dynamics a notch higher. He has found a way of matching the possibilities of orchestral doubling or of organ registration. Here, too, the student sees why certain muscular adjustments are necessary. It is the asynchronization that compels the hand to shift laterally all the more quickly from register to register.

These muscular adjustments are clarified in exercise (e) by restricting the asynchronization to the one form of ascending pitch. The asynchronization has shortened the time interval for lateral shift and has created the necessity to support the hand while the thumb alternates with the other fingers. By contrasting brackets 1 and 3 with bracket 2, the student can perceive how substitution of the thumb for the fifth finger at bracket 2 facilitates the shift from octave to octave.

Finally, at (f) is the passage as Chopin wrote it. The A-flat and G in parentheses at brackets 4 and 5 bring out the extent of the change from exercise (c). Since the principle of substitution that first appeared at bracket 2 has now been applied to brackets 4 and 5 in the opposite direction, the student will find that the middle octave of the three octaves in which the melody is stated has become the most prominent. At the level of this middle octave, the responsibility for carrying the melody has been divided between the thumb and the fifth finger. However, the substitution that makes the division of responsibility possible has also given the passage a total drive by preventing the formation of short segments of two eighth notes apiece.

Each of these exercises represents one layer of the structure, and as each succeeding layer is superimposed upon the preceding, its contribution to the effect is absorbed into the total. In exercise (a), the tension of the harmony, which is created by the Neapolitan chord and its syncopated location, is taken into account and leads to a particular emphasis upon the second quarter note of the first measure. Comparison of exercises (b) and (c) enables the student to gauge the increased scope and enlarged dynamic effect of 19th-century texture that doubling or shifting registers provides. Exercises (d) and (e) make him aware of the telling rhythmic effect of asynchronizing each chord in eighth notes, which lends excitement and storminess to the passage. Thus, the student is under the influence of the context during the very time when he is practicing rather than afterward. There is no need for a realm beyond practicing because "personal emotion and individuality" can be applied nowhere else than at these points in the structure. One performer may find a better way of emphasizing the harmonic tension or the dynamic scope or the rhythmic vitality. But whatever he discovers can apply only to these layers in the construction of the passage.

There are numerous advantages to applying the context while following steps in the understanding of the structure. The student works more confidently. He is no longer as anxious about his progress and has more patience with preliminary steps. His attitude toward muscular problems is more constructive, too, because layer analysis has shown him precisely where and how they arise. His practicing is not troubled by the sensation that someone else already possesses the skill he is trying to acquire; and, more readily accepting the idea that his performance will differ from others, he is less apt to submerge his own individuality in an effort to outdo.

Layer analysis changes the point of view toward muscular difficulty in another fundamental way. We saw, in the case of Cortot's exercises, that anyone who did not experience the muscular difficulty need not do them. Layer analysis, on the contrary, must be done by artist and student alike. Since the rendition results from superimposing each layer on the preceding and from adjusting to the context at each of these stages, no one is excused from following the order of steps that layer analysis dictates. Some players may cover the steps more quickly and acquire the muscular control sooner. But there is no need to hurry. The work with layers of structure is the performance, and when the last layer has been superimposed the work has ended.

From the vantage of this altered attitude toward muscular difficulty, why a fugue often creates more muscular problems than a concert etude becomes clear. In a fugue, the composer condenses what he has to say to a high degree. Fugues therefore entail many superimpositions of layers and detailed, arduous adaptations to the context. Such circumstances suggest a new set of criteria for judging musical accomplishments. A player's muscular control is proportional to how well he applies the music's context, and the passage's difficulty is proportional to how much resistance it offers to applying the context.

One cannot generalize to the extent of saying that later exercises in the series of steps involve greater muscular adjustment than the earlier ones do. In the case of Fig. 10, the amount of adjustment is affected by the type of asynchronization, by the placement of the registers, by the formation of the keyboard surface that happens to lie under the hand grasp, etc. In short, the degree of muscular adjustment will vary with what each succeeding layer brings into play. However, in connection with the allotment of touches defined by Matthay and because layer analysis decides just where they are appropriate, we can say that arm motions will tend to be required during the earlier steps that are near the background, wrist motions in the inter-mediate steps associated with the middleground, and finger motions in the foreground itself.

13 THE FOREGROUND AS THE PRIMARY SOURCE OF UNITY

The first step in the synthesis of the muscular, contextual, and analytic categories has been to construct the exercises on the basis of musical understanding instead of muscular difficulty. The next step is to place the emphasis of analysis-by-reduction on the foreground instead of on the background. As we have said, Schenker traces the unity of a composition to the presence of a minimum melodic and harmonic progression in the back-ground. Instead, the synthesized method traces the unity to the selection and arrangement of the components in the fore-ground. This difference of emphasis will become evident from the contrast between Schenker's analysis of the theme in Chopin's Etude in E major, Op. 10, No. 3, Fig. 11,[28] and the foreground analysis of the same theme given in Fig. 12.

FIG. 11
Schenker's analysis of the theme, Chopin's Etude in E major, Op. 10, No. 3

Schenker's purpose in his analysis is to show that the theme of this Etude may be reduced melodically to three notes and harmonically to the progression I—V—I. The unity of the theme, in his view, arises from the presence of this cadence in the background. Examination of the foreground, however, reveals that its elements are specially designed to serve one particular objective—to produce a sensation of motion to and fro. In the synthesized method, this service of the foreground

Fig. 12

components to one objective is the primary source of the theme's unity.

Fig. 12(a) illustrates how the harmonies are arranged to produce an impression of moving back and forth. Staff (b) presents the accompanying figure in sixteenth notes (semiquavers), (d) the syncopated figure of the bass, and (e) the quarter-note roots of the harmony. All of these elements contribute to the rocking effect. The melody, in staff (c), is also constructed to enhance the oscillatory sensation. During measures 1 and 2 and the first half of 3, the to-and-fro motion

results from neighbouring tones (marked N) and accented
suspensions (As). (It is also possible to analyze the sixteenths
in measures 2 and 3 as anticipations of neighboring tones, but
the oscillatory result would be the same.) Beginning at the
asterisk, appoggiaturas (App.) and accented passing tones (Ap.)
take over the purpose of providing the back-and-forth motion,
and the neighboring tone returns in measure 5. Since appoggiaturas and accented passing tones have a more intense effect

FIG. 13

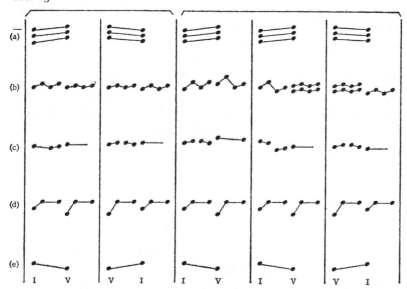

than neighboring tones do, the oscillation of the melodic line
becomes all the more evident in the second half of measure 3
and in measure 4 (notice, also, the expansion of the sixteenth-
note figure of staff (b) at this point in the theme) and then
resumes its initial form. It is no accident that this heightening
of the melody's rocking motion coincides with the climax of the
theme and prompts the insertion of measure 4, thus lengthening
the theme to five measures and departing from the symmetrical arrangement of the harmonies that appeared at the
beginning.

These components of the foreground are presented in Fig. 13 in diagrammatic form. The dots represent the notes and the connecting lines their melodic direction. Such a diagram demonstrates in a graphic way the composer's intention to build a musical structure out of elements that serve one common objective. Music provides him with a variety of materials, such as melodic line, harmonic progression, rhythmic pattern, texture (in this case, so-called melody versus accompaniment), and tone color, which are capable of serving an infinite number of purposes in expression. The composer takes these materials and imposes designs on them so that they all contribute to one objective in expression. This objective is "the central purpose" that we discussed in the preceding chapter and that was detected with the aid of evidence from a variety of sources. We also said there that its presence must be validated by the structure of the composition, and we can now see that the performer finds this validation in the selection and arrangement of the foreground elements.

14　The Canon of Appropriateness

In arriving at the fusion of the central purpose of a composition with its foreground elements, we come upon certain problems that are contained in the idea of tone painting. The term *tone painting* is commonly used to denote relation between the actual world and the world of music, and this is the sense in which we are referring to it. Since the clues to the central purpose are drawn from such sources as titles, accompanying lines of poetry, and biography, they originate in the actual world, whereas the clues to the common objective of the foreground elements come from the musical structure. In order to align and fuse these two types of clues, we must explain precisely how the actual world and the world of music come into relation. We have said that Cortot did not deal with this problem. In evaluating his contribution (Section 10), we pointed out that the right to include the contextual category in a method depends on showing how experience of the actual world is reflected in the world of music and reflected in a way that permits varied interpretation. We must therefore pause in our analysis of musical examples and engage briefly in an aesthetic discussion of the relation between these two worlds.[29] We can then return better equipped to illustrate, in a musical example, how the influence of the context guides the performer toward a perception of compatibility among the foreground's elements.

In general, attempts to relate the actual and the musical worlds run aground for two reasons. First, they do not make sufficient distinction between the possibilities offered by musical materials and the composer's manipulation of these materials. The two factors, manipulation and possibilities, are often confused and the confusion arises because each of them obeys different laws without disobeying the other's. The composer arranges his components in the foreground according to laws of composition. Meanwhile, musical materials have their own laws and organization which the composer also observes. The effect of this situation is to make the possibilities of musical materials more obvious and, correspondingly, to conceal their manipulation by the composer. We know that someone has placed and arranged those components in the foreground, but, since they relate to one another according to the laws of music, it looks as if they arrived there unaided.

Perhaps this situation will become clearer from an analogy with the game of chess. Here, too, the opponent's intention— his manipulation of the chess pieces—is at first obscure, because these pieces are law abiding, because they seem to be governed only by the conditions under which they can move. But there could be no game if the chess player did nothing more than make moves that were law abiding. He does indeed do more. He creates, among consecutive moves, a further relationship that is a design for attack or defense, preferably over as long a series of moves as possible. When the other player perceives this further relationship, he becomes aware of his opponent's intention and acts accordingly. The important thing to notice in this analogy, for its bearing on art, is that anyone can make the move in chess, because it obeys preordained laws, but not everyone could *select* it. Selection and arrangement, whether in chess or in art, signify that intention is present, and we must never let the obedience of the materials to law obscure the fact that someone selected and arranged them. Someone manipulated certain materials in a new way, and if others later followed his example, we should not refer to it as a "discovery" of what was always there and forget that it resulted originally from his intention.

Secondly, the effort to relate the actual world to the world of music is hampered by the vague generality of the term "actual world." Such a world is at worst chaotic and at best prosaic. From birth on, however, man experiences a world that is already clearly ordered and highly organized not only on the basis of function but also, what is most important for our topic, according to a *canon of appropriateness*. Gay occasions bring out liveliness, energy, bright colors; sad occasions call for slow movement and somber colors. A formal dinner suggests one costume, a picnic another. The furnishings of a living room show a certain severity; a kitchen has gleaming surfaces and bright light. In a great many ways, man surrounds his activities with elements that belong to them on the basis of appropriateness. To apply the term we have been using, this disposition of man provides *contexts* for the events and conditions of his life.

Even if the arts did not exist, appropriateness would still dictate man's arrangement of his environment. Noise, violent movement, excitement are appropriate to war; quiet, relaxation, calm are appropriate to peace. The arts simply continue the same effort of arrangement, and therein lies the relation between the actual world and the world of music. The two worlds are related because both undergo selection and arrangement according to the same principle. Thus, when Cortot finds in Chopin's Twelfth Etude "a sublime cry of revolt," we must allow him his interpretation because noise, violent movement, and excitement, which are manifest in its foreground segments, have already been granted in the actual world to be characteristic of revolt. The title that an interpreter gives to a piece of music is his link between an appropriateness within the music and an appropriateness in the actual world. It can serve him either as an aid to finding the appropriateness or as a conviction that he has found it.

The essence of appropriateness is not only in the attachment of particular elements to occasions or situations but also in the exclusion of all other elements. In some areas, white is the color of mourning, in others black. But in the same area, it is rare to use both for this purpose, and in any case, others, like red or green, are excluded. While the reasons for wearing white or black at occasions for mourning may vary, the important consideration is to exclude other colors and, preferably, to attach them to contrasting occasions. For example, where Death calls for black, Life might call for green. The essential requirement on these occasions is to distinguish between Death and Life, and therefore the choice of colours for each must be mutually exclusive.

The endeavor to find the appropriate, then, always contains the need to differentiate, and, when both are fulfilled-man obtains the stability that he demands of his environment. He neither requires nor desires from music representation of the actual world. He looks to music for an orderly, noncontradictory arrangement according to the canon of appropriateness. Thus, context in music does not refer to the actual world but to the orderly arrangements that are suggested to man by the actual world. They become possible in music because its materials lend themselves readily to the detection of similarity and contrast. If forceful accent, widely spaced pitch intervals, and rapidly succeeding notes form a group of mutually appropriate elements, then uniform intensity, small pitch intervals, and slow succession are available to form a contrasting group. These groups are not required to represent the actual world; their formation is justified by experience of the actual world.

Violent excitement and quiet are not experienced together, nor are noise and calm. One does not serenade the beloved with a bugle or call troops together with a guitar.

This resolution of the meaning of tone painting permits the synthesis of method to move much more freely between the contextual and the analytic, between vivid, poetic description and layer analysis by reduction. We can now return to an example in music and show how the canon of appropriateness acts as a guide to the compatibility of the elements of the foreground and permits an estimate of the usefulness to an interpretation of various possible reductions into the background.

In his striking description of Chopin's First Prelude, Cortot wrote of "its impassioned élan and quickened ardor," of its "breathless and feverish" quality, progressing "ever upward" until it reaches "a climax of exaltation," only to subside into a state that "may be likened to the palpitations of a heart overcome by emotion." [30] These are the elements of his interpretation. Perhaps another interpretation of the Prelude would find different elements, but we must agree that, in human experience, "impassioned élan" could be "breathless," could reach "a climax of exaltation" and subside into "palpitations." We must also agree that the context he proposes is not alien to the features of Chopin's music in general. That we form such judgments about a composer's music is attested by our unwillingness to accept this context for the music of Bach or of Mendelssohn. We have said that the endeavor to find the appropriate always contains the need to differentiate and therefore to exclude the contrasting. Let us see, then, what would result if this Prelude were to be interpreted as gentle instead of impassioned.

In Fig. 14(a), the foreground melody has been reduced in one possible way. It has been given one continuous line by joining its separated segments and removing their syncopated rhythm. This alteration gives the first eight measures a gentle, undulating character, as if Chopin intended to write a pleasant, lilting dance. However, he did not develop the lilt of these eight measures in the remaining twenty-six measures of this short piece. That is the important criterion, because any attempt to impose a gentle character on the subsequent material will be defeated. This realization sends us back to the reduction in (a) which we now see as indicating the total arc of the

FIG. 14
Prelude, Op. 28, No. 1, by Chopin

melody rather than its character. We also perceive why Chopin segmented the melody: The segmentation will actually block a lilting effect, and for this purpose, as Fig. 14(b) shows, he has placed a rest at the beginning of each measure and has reinforced the second half of each measure with octaves. Thus, an effort of layer analysis to support the supposed appropriateness of a gentle, lilting character to this Prelude breaks down, and a new direction must be sought.

The clue to this new direction is supplied by the quick, melodic rise of measures 3 and 4, which the composer develops throughout the Prelude. Fig. 14(c) shows that Chopin projected a design in rising and falling intervals of a fourth. In so short a composition, as this different reduction reveals, the rising and falling intervals, occurring every four measures, give it a strong, driving force. They are placed in such a way, likewise, that they prevent any resolution until the very end of the piece, and at the close of the fourth four-measure group (measures 15 and 16), where one might expect a feeling of rest, a modulation to the subdominant propels the music abruptly forward. Then, in measure 18, Fig. 14(d), Chopin discards the silence or rest at the beginning of each measure and puts the melody on the downbeats, thus heightening the momentum still further.

In this way, the layer analysis into rising and falling fourths has supported Cortot's contextual description: The "breathlessness" is identified with the comma or rest at the beginning of each measure; the "impassioned élan" derives from the driving force or momentum of the music; the movement "ever upward" to a "climax of exaltation" is provided by the rising fourths, which span an octave and a half in the space of twenty measures; the "palpitations" result from the two-measure, synoptic version in the coda of what required eight measures at the outset. The qualities of a context that have been validated by experience in the actual world are matched by the qualities that are given off by the elements in the music's foreground.

It is possible, of course, for different performers to arrive at different contextual descriptions of this Prelude. However, as the foregoing analysis shows, they are limited by the necessity to match an appropriateness among the elements of its foreground with an appropriateness among the qualities of the contexts that they have selected. The interpretation of the Prelude as a lilting dance would create glaring inconsistencies and incongruities in its structure. It would also cast doubt on the validity of the experience from which the context was derived: Lilting dances are not danced with driving force. Finally, the composer, on his side, must have chosen mutually appropriate elements for his foreground. Inferior music does not succeed in achieving the requisite appropriateness, but that of the great masters does, and this is precisely why we prize it.

III THE TRANSFORMATION OF PHYSICAL FACTORS FOR THE USES OF PERFORMANCE

15 THE MEANING OF SALIENCE FOR PERFORMANCE

Science, in the form of investigation within the school of objective psychology, has invaded the field of musical performance and reached a startling conclusion: The performer's claim to be able to transmit interpretive aims to the listener is grossly exaggerated. There is indeed a precedent for a different kind of link between science and music, the long-established one that derives from the concern of physics with sound and with the other factors that form the physical basis of music. Sir James Jeans's *Science and Music*, for example, provides a highly effective summary of this relationship under such familiar headings as the analysis of vibration, the design of musical instruments, and the acoustics of concert halls. However, there are no precedents for a scientific evaluation of musical performance. It means venturing beyond the long-standing interdependencies that spring from the physical basis of music and entering the realm of musical aesthetics.

Science finds the stepping stone to this new area in an observation that may be quoted from the same book although it has been stated many times in other sources. Since the piano and its tone depend on certain physical laws, the performer's activity is said to be strictly limited by the operation of those laws: "In striking a single note, the pianist has only one variable at his disposal—the force with which he strikes the key: this determines the velocity with which the hammer hits the wires, and once this is settled, all the rest follows automatically." [31] The scientist then proceeds to demonstrate that a lead weight falling on the key could duplicate both the force of the pianist's finger and the resulting sound wave.

As has happened so often in other fields, the scientific approach presents a formidable challenge by threatening to make customary, long-accepted modes of thought obsolete. Unless we who believe in the power of performance can show (1) that the performer has a working area that conforms with scientific law and (2) that objective psychology has overlooked certain factors that refute its conclusions, we shall be in serious trouble: We shall be forced to admit that the performer's work of interpretation, the arduous and exacting synthesis of method we described in the previous chapter, is so much fanning of the air between him and the listener. He and we would prove to have been victims of our own fond imaginings.

In this chapter, therefore, we shall accept objective psychology's challenge and debate its charges that musical performance is largely self-delusion. Our first step is to prove the need for a change of emphasis. Of the four elements in musical tone—pitch, intensity, duration, and timbre—the investigations have selected and focused attention on intensity. In the case of piano tone, it is easy to see why: The element of intensity is the most clearly and directly related to the use of force on the key, "the only variable at the pianist's disposal." In other words, greater finger force means a stronger hammer blow, causing larger amplitude of string vibration and therefore louder tone. However, the player's concern with tone is not properly described as a judgment of intensity.[32] A much more accurate term for his tonal activity is *judgment of relative salience*: The performer is vitally concerned with how much a tone stands out from or blends with other tones.

Some musical observers, in an effort to counter the scientific limitation of the performer, have pointed out that the relativity of intensity actually gives him enormous latitude. There are no single tones in performance, they say, only tones in relation to other tones, and hence the proviso in Jeans's statement, "in striking a single note," cancels out most of its restricting significance. However, we are not taking refuge in this contention because in proposing the change in emphasis, in replacing the concept of relative intensity with the concept of relative salience, we have gained far more than it could give us. We have discerned a further purpose in the differences in intensity that appear in performance from tone to tone, and we now understand why the performer's execution of this purpose upsets what might confidently be expected of his treatment of intensity.

For example, an accent sign over a given note would seem to be a clear-cut signal to the performer to strike the appropriate key with greater force, thereby giving the note more intensity than the ones surrounding it. Yet there are many times when a performer would actually play such a note with *less* intensity than the surrounding notes because the *conditions* accompanying its appearance in the passage *already rendered it sufficiently salient*. Let us refer to this less immediately explicable behavior of the performer as the *judgment* of a note's *potential for salience*.

What are the conditions that govern a note's potential for salience? Clearly, there are many other factors besides accent signs and they involve all four constituents of tone, pitch, timbre, and duration as well as intensity:

(a) the *place* of a note in such frames as the measure (e.g., on a downbeat rather than an upbeat) and the chord (e.g., being the prime rather than the fifth of a triad);

(b) the *distance* of a note from other notes in the range of pitch (e.g., the potential for salience of notes a fifth apart is different from that of notes one octave plus a fifth apart);

(c) the *register* of a note or its tone color as a result of pitch (e.g., the *chalumeau* or lowest octave of the clarinet as opposed to the same scale two octaves higher);

(d) the relative *dissonance* of a note or the extent to which it clashes with other surrounding notes (e.g., the potential for salience of notes a major seventh apart is different from that of notes a minor second apart);

(e) the relative *consonance* of a note or the extent to which it reinforces other notes or is reinforced by them (e.g., notes in the relation of an octave as opposed to notes in the relation of a fourth);

(f) the *life* of a note or the length of time it has to respond to such conditions as listed above (e.g., the consonant relation of the octave lasting for a whole note as opposed to a quarter note).

Since the four elements—pitch, intensity, duration, and timbre—always act together, never alone, discussing them separately under these six headings is understood to refer to the *manner* in which they serve salience and not to isolated contributions from each. The performer uses them in combination and is able to transform them through the medium of salience and make them responsive to the needs of his performance. His transformation turns them into a kind of code or cryptogram that will defy solution as long as they are defined in purely physical terms. Thus, he will not use more force on the key to make a tone last; he relies on other means besides decibel content to produce increases or decreases in intensity; he does not limit himself to one way of using a given pitch because it always has the same frequency of vibration; he will not feel restricted to the timbre of his own instrument but will find ways to imitate that of other instruments. To the investigator, who has not recognized that this behavior is coded or cryptic, it appears to be trying to set aside physical law. But there is no flouting of physical law. Forces, hidden from the investigation, have intervened to prevent the simplicity of law, at one end of an immense, blurred area, from applying directly to the complexity of performance at the other end.

This complexity, then, this essentially interactive nature of performance, is the extremely important point that the elaborate scientific investigations have managed to overlook. A tone in a musical composition is part of an intricate network of *structural* relationships. Through the activity of performance, changes in structural significance are reflected in variations in the four physical constituents of tone. When these variations are measured by scientific instruments in decibels or vibration patterns or hundredths of a second, they seem to be entirely meaningless and, as such, positive proof that the musical effects they are designed to produce are imaginary. But viewed as the changes in salience that result from the performer's sensitivity to the structural significance of tones, they become not simply comprehensible but highly illuminating. What is more, they change our thinking about tone: The performer should be said to *evoke* tone, not to *produce* it. His evocation will be the joint result of his effort on the key and the passage's conditions of relative salience. He will plan the movement of the key according to his advance estimate of the conditions of relative salience. We shall now describe these conditions for salience in detail.

16 Salience and Physical Intensity

We begin with (a) the *place* of a note. The place of a note in a chord affects the relative salience of its tone. Supposing that it were possible for the four tones of the common chord to receive equal intensity, the soprano would at once obtain a certain salience because it is the topmost tone. Its position makes it distinct, as the ability of a congregation to follow the soprano part of a hymn and not the other parts attests. One may of course point out that soprano salience is decided by the composer's arrangement of the chord and therefore beyond the performer's control. But this contention is irrelevant because there are innumerable occasions when the soprano should not be salient and when the performer will have to compensate for its natural tendency.

The relative salience of a tone is also affected by the place of a note in the measure. Salience increases or decreases according to whether a tone is on the downbeat or on the upbeat. As William James pointed out, "our spontaneous tendency is to break up any monotonously-given series of sounds into some sort of rhythm. We involuntarily accentuate every second, third or fourth beat, and we break the series in still more intricate ways." [33] Each note in a measure serves some purpose in a rhythmic organization and receives a degree of salience thereby. But even independently of rhythm, the order in which a tone appears, its relation to the notes that it precedes and follows, affects its salience. The performer, again, must take into account both the listener's "spontaneous tendency" to give a regular beat to a series of sounds and the conditions of salience in the composer's rhythmic arrangement of notes. Otherwise, his choice of salience will be faulty.

The next factor is (b) the *distance* of a note from its neighbors. The spacing of a tone with relation to others is a determinant of its salience. In general, the farther apart tones are spaced, the greater their degrees of salience. Since all musical tones are organized according to some type of harmonic system, we may say that composers vary spacing of notes by choosing either *close* or *dispersed* position for them. Close position or arranging a series of harmonic notes in their alphabetical order, as A—C—E, emphasizes their effects on consonance. This type of arrangement—the term "close harmony" refers to the same thing—tends to submerge the individuality of tones, and the performer has more difficulty making one or another of them, particularly the inner ones, salient. Distribution of a series of harmonic notes in other than their alphabetical order, as A—E—C, constitutes dispersed or open position, which, conversely, is more favorable for counterpoint. It secures separate and distinct pitch areas for melodic lines and enables them to make their musical points free from interference.

As the number and variety of the conditions for salience increase, it seems all the more remarkable that so demanding and refined a form of judgment must be applied at different levels in the total scale of intensity. Notation employs a system of intensity in which each division supposedly *doubles* the one preceding, as *mf—f—ff* or *mezzo-forte—forte—fortissimo*. "Supposedly *doubles*" is the most one can say, because, in a scientific sense, a geometric series without a clue to a unit is impractical. Nevertheless, the performer knows what this series means. He realizes into sound not only various levels of intensity but also the infinite variety of saliences within each level.

The performer understands what the doubling of dynamics in the series signifies because he uses it to derive the import of the passage and not to refer to actual intensities. His procedure is analogous to that of the reader whom the novelist provides with a graduated scale of dynamics for the purpose of qualifying dialogue: "he said," "he affirmed," "he emphasized," "he shouted," "he screamed." These interpolations help the reader to derive the import of speeches and do not refer to specific degrees of intensity. We have called the performer's apportionment of intensity remarkable in that he is able to retain the same relationships of salience at different levels of intensity or, to use another comparison, in that he accomplishes in sound what the enlargement of a photograph does for sight. Yet the novelist's scale of dynamics reminds us that no one has any difficulty, while repeating the same phrase more loudly or more softly, in still retaining the proper distribution of accents that makes him understood.

We may also mention here, although it will figure importantly later on, another aid to the distribution of salience that the player has. Whenever the listener is under a *continuing* stimulus, he does not become oblivious of it but remains aware of it at a less conscious level. If the music requires one voice or part to be salient, a performer, by emphasizing its first few notes, can draw the listener's attention there and expect him to continue considering it salient until the purpose of the music changes. The performer is meanwhile freed to make other points, provided that the general salience of this voice part is not upset. In the case of an obbligato to a theme that has previously been stated, the pianist can treat the theme as he would a continuing stimulus, and the double demand on salience, namely, the requirement that both the theme and its obbligato be evident, is easier to handle. When waltzes are played, too, the audience comes to expect the standardized waltz bass to continue and soon relegates it to a lower level of consciousness, thereby permitting the performer to distribute the saliences in the treble more freely.

17 FUNCTIONAL AND PHYSICAL PITCH

Still under the headings of the place of a note and its distance from its neighbors, we shall now consider how the factor of pitch figures in the performer's response to the conditions of salience. Pitch is defined in physics mainly in terms of the frequency of vibrations per second. In music, this definition is subordinated to the purposes of the scale and of the intervals of harmony. Every choice of pitch therefore involves a preordained distance from another pitch both when notes are in succession and when they are sounded together. If pitch did not thus provide a preplanned network of relationships, transcription from one key to another would not be possible. Also, earlier music could not have survived the general rise in pitch (about a semitone) that has occurred over the century and a half since Beethoven's time.

Consequently, the performer's response to pitch is not to changes in the frequency of vibration but to compound stimuli in the musical score. It would be incorrect, for example, to assume that the performer always responds to rising or falling pitch by increasing or decreasing intensity of tone. Such a tendency can be indulged to some extent in single-line music like Gregorian chant. Elsewhere, it cannot be applied because melody has been subjected to other, counteractive forces. Some themes are really a cross of two vocal lines and flit from one to the other like a single singer who is trying to convey the idea of a duet. To follow such meanderings with increasing and decreasing intensity would be disturbing. In other themes, the highest notes sometimes occupy positions that are subordinate from a rhythmic point of view. To give them greater intensity because their pitch is higher would disrupt the rhythm.

Let us suppose, however, that a performer has decided to respond to rising and falling pitch with increasing and decreasing intensity and that, for this purpose, he can increase by one degree the intensity of each succeeding note of the scale. Of the eight consecutive notes beginning with A, A would then have 1 degree of intensity; B, 2 degrees; C, 3 degrees, etc. Applying this allotment of degrees of intensity to the theme of Chopin's Berceuse Op. 57, Fig. 15, the following order of intensities would result:

FIG. 15
Berceuse Op. 57, by Chopin

Name of note in the theme:	F	E♭	A♭	F	E♭	F	D♭	B♭	C	E♭	A♭	D♭
Relative height of pitch:	6	5	8	6	5	6	4	2	3	5	1	4
Degree of intensity:	6	5	8	6	5	6	4	2	3	5	1	4

Intensity now corresponds to the height of pitch in the scale and increases and decreases with the contour of the melody. Yet, assigning intensities according to this plan would not prove satisfactory: The highest note, A-flat, which received 8 degrees or the strongest intensity, would stand out too much because it

is in a subordinate rhythmic position and because it is separated
by intervals of a fourth and a third from the notes that precede
and follow it; the second E-flat in the theme, which received 5
degrees of intensity, would emerge stronger than expected because it is on the downbeat. Each tone of the theme would be
affected in ways such as these due to the particular conditions
of salience accompanying its appearance.

These conclusions are borne out by a graph of the intensities
in an actual performance of the theme of this Berceuse.[34] It
was obtained by electronic methods and showed the following
decibel ratings for the measures in Fig. 15:

Name of note in the theme:	F	E♭	A♭	F	E♭	F	D♭	B♭	C	E♭	A♭	D♭
Relative height of pitch:	6	5	8	6	5	6	4	2	3	5	1	4
Decibels:	13	10	3	12	7	10	7	7	1	5	½	7

The highest A-flat has a rating of only 3 decibels, and the
second E-flat measured only 7 decibels although the first
E-flat rated 10 decibels. Clearly, this performer was utilizing
the conditions of salience in conjunction with intensity to
produce what he considered an appropriate curve for the
melody. He treated pitch in terms of its varying functions for
the musical structure rather than in terms of its physical
definition.

It follows from the foregoing results with electronic methods
that a second method of calculating intensity during actual
performance, namely, by measuring the hammer velocities that
were employed, would be completely deceptive.[35] For example,
the performer of the Berceuse must have used greater force of
touch in producing a 10-decibel E-flat than in the case of the
7-decibel E-flat. The measuring device would therefore show
greater hammer velocity for the first E-flat than for the second,
and, when this was translated into intensity, the result might be
a ratio of, let us say, 5 units of intensity to 3. Seeing a rating of
3 units for the second E-flat, a player who wished to imitate the
measured performance would mistakenly conclude that the
intensity of this tone should *appear* to be less than that of the
first E-flat. Although the original pianist was undoubtedly

counting on the downbeat location of the second E-flat to give it sufficient salience, the imitating player would actually be trying to reduce the effect of salience by using less force of touch. In short, to calculate intensity from hammer velocity is to mislead other players about what took place in the original performance. It sets up a scale of intensities that bears no relation to intensities achieved in terms of the conditions of salience.

The performer, then, shares with the composer a structural attitude toward pitch that eludes the direct approach of the measuring device. As he uses intensity to mirror the constantly changing functions of pitch, he occasionally receives suggestions from the composer about where and how to do so. For example, the composer sometimes takes advantage of the leading tone's tendency to resolve upward to the keynote by substituting the deceptive harmonization, dominant to submediant (V to VI), for the perfect cadence, dominant to tonic (V to I), as in Fig. 16(a). He will then frequently mark the submediant *subito piano*, or suddenly soft, in order to emphasize blocking the leading tone, temporarily, from resolving completely. Beethoven was particularly fond of this play on pitch and also of giving unusual emphasis to the dominant in the perfect cadence (V—I) by marking it *sforzando*, or suddenly strong, as in the third excerpt of Fig. 16(a). Another way of utilizing the leading tone's tendency—one which hastens rather than delays resolution—is the anticipation. Arias in oratorios illustrate this device, which causes the melody to reach resolution ahead of the remainder of the chord and suggests the need for a nuance of increasing intensity or for a *crescendo*.

The performer will naturally welcome these suggestions and respond to them. But in the course of music, there are countless other occasions involving degrees of resolution, which are not expressly called to his attention by the composer and which he must discover by himself. To such unspoken requests he responds as well. His realm of action extends to the smallest detail, and when he receives the larger-scale suggestions from the composer, he interprets them as the composer's express wishes for particular ways, among many others, of carrying out functions of pitch.

We can better understand this effort to reflect the composer's structural intent at every turn of phrase or change of pitch if we think of melodies as forces that fluctuate in strength as well

Fig. 16

(a) Concluding measures, Piano Sonata No. 27 in E minor, Op. 90, by Beethoven

The opposite, from Allegro molto, Piano Sonata No. 31 in A-flat major, Op. 110, by Beethoven

Sforzandi on the dominant, from Adagio, Piano Sonata No. 11 in B-flat, Op. 22, by Beethoven

(b) Trio of Aria con Variazioni, by Haydn

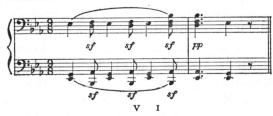

as change direction. In the secondary theme by Haydn, from the Trio of his *Aria con variazioni* in F minor, Fig. 16(b), the force that brings the melody to its fourth note, C, weakens perceptibly during the remaining notes. The energy lessens after C because the next six notes are incidental to its movement to the final A. These six notes decorate the melody in a harmonic way and depart from previous types of ornament due, perhaps, to the advent of the pianoforte. Consequently, the rise in pitch during this ornamental figure has no melodic significance and is simply a by-product of breaking or arpeggiating a chord.

The functions of pitch change, then, as the force of a melody fluctuates in strength. Often, too, these fluctuations in melodic force are accomplished by changes in style. By "style," here, we mean melodic features that are more suited to one instrument than to another. The first four notes of Haydn's theme, for example, would be well suited to the voice, but the remaining notes would torture it and be difficult even for a coloratura soprano. Conversely, the ornamental figure is simple and effective on the piano, whereas the vocal style of the first four notes makes greater demands on the pianist. Such transfer or transcription of styles, despite the difficulties for the performer that result, is extremely common, and any sophisticated melody is truly a compendium of features that originated on a variety of instruments. The "instrumental style" (figuration derived from string and keyboard instruments) of Bach's and Handel's vocal fugues is well known, and the *Song Without Words* is familiar on the pianoforte. Perhaps the ultimate explanation for transcription of style is the tendency of composers to treat melody as melodic line. They become absorbed in the possibilities of an attractive melodic contour and forget that it was originally designed for one particular instrument.

It is this mixture of styles in melody and also in musical structure as a whole that makes the limitations of an instrument less significant and the powers of individual performers more decisive. The essential meaning of virtuosity is an ability to reveal unsuspected possibilities in an instrument, and skill in transcription, such as that of Liszt, is an important stimulus to finding these new possibilities. Similarly, just when people were concluding that Brahms's solos were unpianistic, capable performers proved this to be untrue, and nowadays students toss off his difficulties as a matter of course. Such accomplishments encouraged the transcription of styles still further, and composers became more and more confident that the performer would use his instrument's greater resources in one respect to compensate for its deficiencies in another.

This kind of remedial compensation by the performer is of great help to the composer. It permits him, for example, to give the same theme alternately to different instruments in chamber and orchestral music. He can behave identically toward instruments of fixed and variable pitch. Although the pitch of keyboard instruments is fixed and that of string instruments variable, he can shift the same theme from the piano to the violin. He is counting on the keyboard players to substitute the strong points of their instrument for the weak, like the blind who perform the functions of sight with an acute ear and a sensitive touch. The clavichord has a small tone but it can nuance or graduate intensity. The harpsichord cannot nuance but it offers octave coupling or the playing of notes one or more octaves apart with a single finger. The organ has its stops or varieties of tone color to balance its uniformity of intensity. And while the piano does not have stops or octave couplers, it offers the immense resources of keyboard touch.

No one instrumentalist is enabled to meet all the demands of music by the construction of his instrument alone. The violinist can indeed create pitch, but he has had to learn to extend a limited range by means of harmonics and the high positions and to overcome discomfort in playing chords through ingenious devices of arpeggiation. The composer has been freed to transcribe styles not as much by the capacities of an instrument as by the performer's adaptation of them. He can center his attention on functions within the musical structure because

he can depend on the player to make their significance evident
to the listener.

18 SYNTHETIC, THEMATIC, AND PHYSICAL TIMBRE

This section is concerned with heading (c), the *register* of a note,
that is, its particular tone color within the characteristic timbre
of an instrument. Different areas or registers of an instrument's
pitch range have recognizable qualities or tone colors. For
example, Beethoven, in such works as the Piano Concerto
No. 4 in G major, Op. 58, and the Piano Sonata No. 32 in C
minor, Op. 111, pioneered a wide dispersal of tones and in
some extreme instances placed the pianist's hands at opposite
ends of the keyboard. Placing the left hand of the player in the
rich, low register and his right hand in the thin, high register
will markedly differentiate the tasks of each on the basis of
timbre. As a rule, the farther apart two tones are, the more
independent of differences in intensity their salience can be.

The entire subject of timbre was first investigated systematic-
ally by Hermann von Helmholtz (1821–94) in his *Sensations of
Tone* (1862). His theories are based on the fact that when a
string vibrates, it vibrates in equal segments in addition to
vibrating as a whole, and these segments produce tones of
their own that are absorbed into the total impression. Such
tones are called "upper partials" (sometimes "overtones" and
"harmonics") because they contribute to the tone's effect and
are higher in pitch than the prime that gives the note its name.
They form the "harmonic series," and in the range of pitch
above the prime the first partial will lie an octave higher; the
second, a fifth beyond; the third, two octaves higher; and the
fourth, a third beyond. Therefore, these upper partials, which
are only the first few in a long series, span two octaves and a
third above the prime and are produced by the subdivision of
the string into two, three, four, and five equal segments respectively.

Helmholtz traced the quality or timbre of a tone to the presence and prominence of particular upper partials. We are able to tell the tone of a violin from that of a flute because the violin's remote partials are more prominent, and we can differentiate between a flute and a clarinet because in the flute's tone the second and third partials predominate and in the clarinet's the alternate ones. The physical definition of timbre, then, refers to the particular tone color of an instrument and ascribes it to the arrangement and strength of the upper partials. Since such differences among the upper partials occur from section to section of an instrument's pitch range, they create registers that influence the salience of the tones belonging to each section.

Heading (d) deals with the relative *dissonance* of a note or the extent to which it clashes with its surroundings. In another phase of his experiments, Helmholtz showed that the upper partials of one tone can conflict with those of another, producing a disturbance called "beats," which the ear considers tonally unpleasant or dissonant. Utilizing this definition for our present purpose, we may say that if several tones surround such a dissonant tone and are pleasant sounding or consonant, it will gain salience from the contrast. Illustrations of the principle of salience due to contrast are so numerous in other areas besides the art of music that it needs no introduction. They range from the black sheep to Wordsworth's "Fair as a star when only one is shining in the sky." How salient a dissonant tone becomes by comparison with others depends upon a judgment of the severity of the dissonance and the degree of surrounding consonance. Judgment of dissonance is a subtle matter requiring fine discrimination, particularly where music of earlier times is concerned. The performer must take himself back to a time when an interval that he has become accustomed to consider relatively consonant was felt as a dissonance. Here again, salience as a result of the factor of dissonance needs less assistance from intensity.

The relative *consonance* of a note, (e), depends upon the

extent to which it reinforces other notes or is reinforced by them. A third phase of Helmholtz's work was concerned with musical intervals and the phenomenon of "reinforcement." When a tone and the octave above it are sounded, some of the partials of both tones will coincide and reinforce each other. For example, the first partial of the lower tone will coincide with the prime of the tone an octave above, and the third partial of the lower tone will reinforce the first partial of the higher tone. [36] This factor of mutual reinforcement is of great importance to the present discussion and we shall give the result it produces the special term "synthetic timbre." We are calling the mutual reinforcement of intervals in performance *synthetic* timbre because the listener is conscious that *both tones* of the interval have been played, whereas in the case of *physical* timbre he is conscious of *only one tone*, the partials having merged into one total impression.

We cannot emphasize too much that such reinforcement takes place without the aid of the damper pedal and is solely due to coincidence of partials. [37] Naturally, raising all the dampers and freeing strings for "sympathetic vibration" will produce additional patterns of reinforcement. But to suppose that mutual reinforcement depends exclusively on the damper pedal is to overlook the reinforcement that musical intervals themselves produce and that is proportional to their degrees of consonance. Whenever a pianist performs a passage without using the damper pedal, he has decided that the patterns of reinforcement provided by the musical intervals are sufficiently suited to his purpose and that additional reinforcement from the pedal might interfere with their effect. In reality, he returns to the situation of the harpsichordist and clavichordist who did not have the use of a damper pedal and who yet took full advantage of the reinforcement of intervals and the resulting saliences. For example, they employed the "organ point," a tone held throughout changes of chords: The opposing notes that were in consonant relation with the held tone refurbished or recalled it sufficiently.

The effect of synthetic timbre on the common chord is to create new conditions of salience. If the reader will try on the piano each of the three chords in Fig. 17, sounding all the notes as nearly as possible with equal force, he will notice that the changes in the bass staff alter the salience of the treble tones: The tenor of the first chord will become more salient by coincidence with the fourth partial of the bass, which in this instance is especially strong; the alto of the second chord will be particularly reinforced by the second partial of the bass; and the soprano of the third chord will gain in salience from reinforcement by the first partial of the bass. These varying conditions for salience must be taken into account by the performer, just as he does where position, location, and register are concerned. Since the demands of musical structure will at

FIG. 17

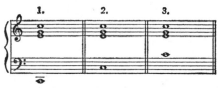

different times require the performer to give salience to each part in such four-note chords, the reader should try, first, to bring out the soprano in each chord, then the alto, the tenor, and the bass. He will be convinced that the conditions of salience created by one distribution of chordal tones cannot equally favor each attempt to bring out a part. We must distinguish, therefore, between the composer's demands for salience and the existing conditions of salience. We must say that the performer has the task of adjusting touch and tone to the *musical* conditions of salience under the *physical* conditions of salience.

Following up Beethoven's pioneering dispersal of notes of chords, the 19th-century composers gave more attention to this aspect of the performer's task. They became more aware of a possible collision between their musical demands and the predisposed conditions of salience that make for synthetic timbre.

What would result, they asked themselves, if musical demands were made *in terms of* predisposed conditions of salience? They found the logical answer in arranging the notes of chords in imitation of the distribution of upper partials within the harmonic series. Recognizing that physical timbre depends upon the harmonic series they created a great variety of synthetic or artificial timbres by duplicating the distribution of the partials with the aid of actually sounded tones. Thus, they greatly expanded the possibilities of synthetic timbre, which we have shown to be inherent in the system of musical intervals, producing all sorts of new timbre effects by artificial imitation of the harmonic series.

This 19th-century development reached a climax in the music of Debussy. In the following theme from *Jimbo's Lullaby* (from *The Children's Corner*), Fig. 18(a), Debussy chose the low

FIG. 18
Jimbo's Lullaby, from The Children's Corner, by Debussy

register of the piano to capture an impression of the elephant's slow-moving gait. Tones of low pitch are suited to slow movement because they tend to become indistinct when they change rapidly. First stated unaccompanied, the theme shifts to the middle register where it threatens to lose its "soft and somewhat awkward" character. The composer, accordingly, harmonizes the melody as follows: Fig. 18(b). Notice how the distribution of the notes follows the example of the harmonic series. Fig. 18(c) shows the net effect of synthetic timbre. Many pianists

FIG. 19

Passage from Piano Concerto No. 5 in F major, Op. 103, by Saint-Saëns

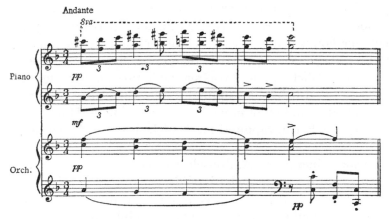

intensify it by performing the passage with the damper pedal depressed throughout.

As the excerpt from Debussy reveals, synthetic timbre may be manufactured at various degrees of asynchronization as well as in chords, and the effects depend on how closely the artificial distributions resemble the actual models for timbre in nature. Sometimes the imitation is particularly faithful: Fig. 19. In this passage from his Piano Concerto No. 5 in F major, Op. 103, Saint-Saëns keeps strictly to the intervals of the twelfth and the eighteenth, as derived from the harmonic series—some organ stops do the same thing—and he thereby emphasizes the merging of upper with lower tones that is typical of physical timbre.

These examples also show that the effect of synthetic timbre is stronger when the various melodic lines in the musical structure are predominantly parallel or when the same tones are repeated again and again from measure to measure. The nature of timbre itself is responsible for this circumstance in that it needs a fairly long time to make a definite impression. Parallel melodic lines and extended repetition of notes become signals to performers that the composer is trying to produce synthetic timbre, and they will respond by evaluating intensities vertically or harmonically instead of horizontally or melodically. If parallel writing prevails, they will treat only one of the voices melodically and subordinate the others to it. If the repeated-note method is being used, they will reiterate the tones merely to keep them sounding rather than curve them into melodies.

Since parallel motion favors synthetic timbre, one might not expect to find it in contrapuntal music where the voices have individuality and often move in contrary motion. However, in the supremely contrapuntal music of J. S. Bach, the harmonic factor is never lost sight of, no matter how complex the weaving of melodic lines becomes. Pre-selected successions of chords, the *continuo*, are always at the basis of his structures. For this reason, the difference between his preludes and his fugues or between his chorales and his chorale preludes is mainly one of emphasis. It is easier to derive the harmony in the preludes and the chorales. The fugues and the chorale preludes have many more superimposed layers, but when they are reduced by harmonic analysis they are found to obey the same harmonic principles that the preludes and chorales do. The key to synthetic timbre in Bach's music, therefore, lies in the distribution of the tones that carry out the basic harmonic progressions.

When a performer plays Bach or other contrapuntal music, he first estimates how near the surface the harmonic progression lies. If there are few layers between the foreground and the progression, this is a sign that the notes are to be treated less

FIG. 20
Fantaisie, from Partita No. 3 in A minor, by Bach

melodically. In Fig. 20, for example, Bach's original thematic line, (a), has been altered into (b) in order to reduce the number of layers and make the harmony more evident. When playing (b), the performer will give less importance to the progress from one sixteenth note to the next. But even when he plays (a), his awareness of the underlying rhythm will cause him to draw attention to the distribution of the tones in an implied chord. He thus produces an effect of synthetic timbre. That this effect is real and individual may be proved by altering the distribution of harmonic tones according to (c), which will result in a different and equally recognizable effect of synthetic timbre.

Effects of synthetic timbre, then, have existed ever since the time when melodic lines were first combined. They are simply less obvious and less colorful because a limited pitch range tended to confine them to the middle register. A true extension of the range of pitch came toward the end of the 18th century, and it was then that composers conceived the idea of imitating the harmonic series. New possibilities were offered by new registers and the middle register became gray by comparison. It lost color, too, from association with harmony exercises and other study materials, which often lie in the middle register and in close position besides. To discover the synthetic timbre in earlier music, therefore, the performer must seek a mean between the one extreme of neutral color and the other of dazzling effect. He will find that synthetic timbre is not only present but also richly rewarding.

There is a second kind of timbre that also enables the performer to outreach the physical limitations of an instrument's tone color. We shall call this type of timbre *thematic*. As we have stated, a melody most often derives from the possibilities of several instruments. Also, composers do not hesitate to shift it, unchanged, from one instrument to another. To have become indebted to several instruments and to be playable interchangeably, melodic contour, at its beginnings, must have been simple and must have reflected the main capacity of a single instrument. Illustrations of such simple melodies are horn calls, trumpet fanfares, birdlike trills on the flute, and oriental scales on the oboe. These have existed to the present day.

Not only are the calls and fanfares ideally suited to the instruments that originated them but they also continue to retain their association with the purposes they once served. Indeed, their melodic contours are so distinctive that they can be played on other instruments and not lose their character. On the piano, for example, a horn call is so effective that it evokes both the spirit of the call and the timbre of the horn. Despite the fact that the pianist is using different and less-suited resources, the melodic outline of the horn call exerts a powerful influence and creates the impression that the timbre of the horn has been reproduced. *Thematic timbre*, then, is the power of certain melodic contours to recall the instruments that originated them.

Only certain kinds of instruments, however, are suited to the purpose of thematic timbre. Their timbre has a special flexibility that permits transfer of the call or fanfare: they convey the transferred quality without obtruding their own. Among such instruments are the voice, the piano, the strings, and the clarinet, but not the celesta and the xylophone. The flute and the oboe are borderline cases. When the timbres of instruments are too specific to subordinate themselves, the listener hears only their typical sound. This circumstance suggests a division of instruments into two classes, *solo* and *occasional*. A *solo instrument* is one that permits thematic timbre, that allows a theme to recall other instruments and the ideas associated with them. An *occasional instrument* remains itself under all conditions and can be used only as its own timbre dictates.

There has been difference of opinion whether an instrument belongs in the one class or the other. Late in the 19th century, Brahms was still treating the trumpet as an occasional instrument, that is, largely for martial purposes, whereas the French composers and Wagner had given it solo status. The controversy over the relative merits of the natural horn and the valve horn arose from the same source: The proponents of the natural horn wished the horn to remain an occasional instrument and not be made to serve a variety of expressive aims. For a similar reason, the saxophone has not become a standard symphonic instrument; its timbre is considered by many composers to be too specialized for inclusion in what we have termed the solo category.

Once an instrument is accepted into the solo class, it can utilize the stylized melodic contours and assume responsibilities that the occasional instrument ordinarily fulfills. At first, the composer's skill with thematic timbre is limited to the more obvious instances, the horn calls, fanfares, trills, and oriental

scales. Later on he progresses from the horn call to a haunting
nostalgia, from a fanfare to the heroic spirit, from birdlike
trills to the pastoral, and from the oriental to the melancholy
and desolate: Fig. 21(a), (b), (c), (d), respectively. But however subtly the composer transmutes bald imitations of instruments into delicate evocations of mood, his success ultimately

FIG. 21

(a) Measures 6–8, Der Lindenbaum, by Schubert

(b) Passage from Novellette, Op. 21, No. 8, by Schumann

(c) Measures 15–16, Bruyeres, by Debussy

(d) Measures 73–76, Mazurka in C-sharp minor, Op. 41, No. 1, by Chopin

depends on the ability of the performer to adapt the timbre of the solo instrument to those purposes.

19 STRUCTURAL AND PHYSICAL DURATION

Finally, among the conditions that make for relative salience is (f), the *life* of a note. The salience of a note is affected by its duration or the length of time it has to respond to the five other conditions of salience that we have discussed. In performance, duration is treated in terms of function for musical structure. From a physical point of view, one might expect to define the duration of a tone as the length of time it lasts, but this definition is not applicable to music. Three circumstances should convince us of the truth of this statement. First, pianoforte tone dies out very quickly, that of the harpsichord and the clavichord even sooner. Physically, such tone would offer poor assistance to the purposes of duration, and yet, duration plays as much of a part, indeed, much the same part, in music for these instruments as it does elsewhere.

Second, if duration in music depended on how long a tone lasted, the whole notes and half notes in pianoforte music would tend to be marked *forte*. That is, since a stronger blow of the hammer would make the sound of a tone last longer, the composer could be expected to anticipate the need to mark notes of longer duration to be played more strongly. The actual situation is precisely the opposite. The slow movements of sonatas, where long duration is the rule, are most often marked *pianissimo*, and it is music in an *allegro vivace* or *presto* tempo that has the most *forte* and *fortissimo* signs.

Third, the nonphysical nature of duration in music is confirmed in a very significant way by the presence of "rests." Rests, which also have duration values, silence tone completely. Yet, the function of duration for musical structure is understood to go on during the rest, the listener being expected to pick up the thread of the music, when tone begins again, from the point where it left off. The thirteenth variation in Beethoven's *Variations on a Waltz of Diabelli*, Op. 120, Fig. 22, is an extraordinary illustration of how the thread of meaning continues during long rests. It also testifies to Beethoven's mastery of the purposes of silent duration.

Duration in music, therefore, does not depend upon the sustaining power of tone. It depends upon a note's structural

FIG. 22

Variation XIII, Thirty-three Variations on a Waltz of Diabelli, Op. 120, by Beethoven

purpose. For example, in Fig. 23(a), the half note A has the function of an appoggiatura, or accented, unprepared dissonance, which is resolved at the quarter note G. Throughout this half note, there is a state of tension that is created by the conflict of the suddenly appearing dissonance with the consonances accompanying it and that is not relieved until the arrival of the consonant note G. To define the duration as performance uses it, we must say that tension caused by an appoggiatura lasted a half note, not that the tone lasted a half note. We commonly make the same kind of distinction in ordinary experience. On one occasion we say, "The train was an hour late," and on another, "The jury reached a verdict in an hour." We use the same duration term, "an hour," on both occasions, but we by no means mean the same thing. In the case of the train, we mean that the delay was long; regarding the jury, we mean that its deliberation was short. Our discrimination between an hour's time and what transpires within it is analogous to the difference between physical and structural duration in music.

The appoggiatura, of course, is only one of the many functions for musical structure that a note can have. At Fig. 23(b), the same note, A, has a different significance. Coming at the very start of a composition and being part of a tonic chord, it suggests that tenser relations are to come and awaits explanation by the remainder of the piece. The purpose of its duration, structurally, is to create expectation of what is to ensue. This purpose is furthered by the preceding tone, C, since the function

FIG. 23

(a)   (b)

of an upbeat is to help define the structural duration of the initial, frequently tonic, chord. That the structural duration of the note that begins the piece is carefully calculated, despite its apparently bland, neutral character, is illustrated by Fig. 24. This figure shows what would occur if the first melodic note in Schubert's Impromptu in G-flat, Op. 90, No. 3, were lengthened to four times its original duration. Whether played on the piano or on the organ, the B-flat is now unsuited to begin the main theme. Thus elongated, the passage might serve as an introduction, but the initial note can no longer open a melody because it disappoints the expectation of what might follow. We see once more that structural duration is calculated independently of the sustaining power of tone.

The contribution that a note makes to structural duration has a strong effect on its potential for salience. For this reason, composers prefer Fig. 25(a) to (b) despite the fact that in (b) the top tones of the bass figure reinforce the soprano. When a

FIG. 24

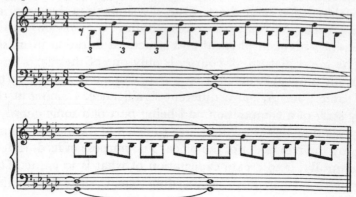

note is not doubled, it has the entire responsibility for a function in the structure and stands out from the others by virtue of this distinction. J. S. Bach observes the principle of nonduplication extremely strictly and, as a result, his music is a model for the highly desirable features of "economy of means" and "inevitability of statement." By giving each note a separate function for the structure, he needs only a few notes to express his purpose and then they seem exactly right for that purpose.

In conclusion, the functions of notes for the structure of a piece enable the composer to allot their durations. As he works on the structure, he feels the need for a neighboring tone here and a passing tone there, and on second thought he may change them from eighth notes to quarters. He estimates their contributions to his structure, and the durations he eventually gives them represent the lengths of time he thinks they need in order to make those contributions. The performer, for his part, comes to recognize what the functions of the notes signify and why

FIG. 25

they need their allotted durations. He then creates for them a pattern of saliences that in his opinion permits the listener to grasp their significance.

20 SALIENCE AND THE CONTEXT

We must now discuss a second type of salience which, for the sake of avoiding confusion, we have thus far not considered. I refer on a smaller scale to the characteristics that dominate a passage and that are described in the musical score by such terms as *dolce, dolente, espressivo,* etc. and, on a larger, to the connotation of the composition as a whole, the sort of total impression that led Beethoven to call his eighth piano sonata *Pathétique* and his third symphony *Eroica.* Clearly, this second type of salience is an extension of the first type and follows from enlargement of the units that are brought into relation. The process of relating larger and larger units takes the box-within-box form in music and occurs in two directions, "horizontal" and "vertical." Horizontally, the progression is from note to motif to phrase to section to movement. Vertically, the notes group into counterpoints, harmonic or accompaniment figures, basso continuos, etc. The two types of salience, then, are completely interdependent. Characteristics of the passage and other larger units become salient as a result of the saliences among tones, and saliences among tones are selected according to their usefulness in revealing the salient characteristics of the passage and the other larger units.

"To reveal the salient" seems like a contradiction in terms until we remember that we are discussing a developmental activity that leads to and culminates in the synthesis of method. The salient characteristics of a passage are not self-evident; they only seem that way after it has been satisfactorily performed. They must be detected by the performer, and for this purpose he searches for relations between structural components and progressively larger units of characteristics that define the context of the music. The context or expressive content of a passage is far from being a general character that has been stamped upon an agglomeration of notes. On the contrary, the composer breaks up the context into elements. He could not otherwise present his music understandably, and, as a logical result, he associates each element of the context with a component of the musical structure. The performer, then, works in the reverse order, and, deriving from the structural components those elements of the context that the composer has allotted to them, relates the elements to each other as he relates the structural components to each other. He thus forms an idea of the passage's context or expressive content.

We can perceive clearly how the performer succeeds in relating structural components to contextual elements if we are careful to differentiate between the means, the abstract possibilities of musical structure, and the end, the concrete, actual structure of a particular composition. The means is restricted in the sense that it remains the same, but it is unrestricted through its adaptability to a variety of ends. The sameness of the component is compensated for by a freedom to choose among the many possible functions it can have as part of a structure. For example, although the accent in 3/4 time is usually on the first quarter note, musical structure permits it to be displaced to the second or third quarter. Therefore, when an accent on, let us say, the second quarter appears in the musical score, it signifies a decision by the composer. He has chosen one among the three possibilities. Should he then go further and place two eighth notes on the first quarter and a chord in half notes on the remaining quarters, as in Fig. 26, he has, in effect, assembled components of *a* musical structure because they are among the possible components of musical structure.

As selection signifies decision, so decision implies purpose, and, if all the decisions can be correlated, they may be said to have a common purpose. When the structural components in Fig. 26 are examined closely, they show a common purpose.

They all contribute to accent on the second quarter. Notice how the stoppage of melodic motion on the dotted quarter notes and, in the second measure, the ties before entry of the chord emphasize the second quarters of the measures. Of course, one must assume that the composer is competent and that he has selected components that structure permits to be combined. But if these two conditions are satisfied, comparison of the structural components will reveal their common purpose, and from this purpose the expressive content of the passage can be deduced. In Fig. 26, the choice of melodic intervals and of chords points toward the same purpose as the emphasis on the second quarter does, and the performer can conclude that

Fig. 26

the composer's intention was to write a sarabande, because the components of the structure reproduce the features that a sarabande requires. Even when the composer supplies the title Sarabande, the performer, in order to justify it, must still reach the same conclusion and in the same way. When the composer does not affix a title, the expressive content of pieces like the excerpt in Fig. 26 will be said to resemble that of a sarabande.

The performer now has before him two aggregates, one, the contextual elements that are comprised under the heading sarabande, and the other, the structural components whose common purpose reveals the composer's intention to write one. He then draws a parallel between the two wholes: As the elements combine to characterize the context, so the components combine to form a musical structure. Relations among the elements suggest to him relations among the components and vice versa. It is this simultaneous concern with the two aggregates that makes the musical structure a meaningful whole rather than merely a correct assemblage. For any one performer, there is one particular set of relationships among the structural components that is above and beyond their obedience to musical law and that lies in their *appropriateness* to one another. Were this not the case and did not the further criterion of appropriateness apply, all manners of rendering the music would appear equally satisfactory to him. He could play it at a certain tempo or at another twice as fast with equally satisfying results. Yet the fact that a sarabande calls for slow movement and seriousness of mood would not in itself decide the issue. Since the composer, before the performer, also held the context in view, a limit has been placed on the conditions under which the structural components will combine into relationships of mutual appropriateness. That is, their mutual appropriateness will be found only when it is sought within the context of slow movement and seriousness of mood.

The discovery of a mutual appropriateness among the structural components is also the discovery of the passage's salient characteristics since each component increases the impression of appropriateness as it contributes to musical structure. To the listener, this mounting impression of appropriateness appears as the context of the music. The performer's success with the listener depends upon how clearly the latter has perceived the context and this, in turn, depends on how completely his attention has been transferred from the components of the musical structure to the elements of the expressive content. Thus, the final goal of the second or larger-unit type of salience is reached, and the listener apprehends the passage in terms of its salient characteristics.

It is worth pausing at this point to ask whether the scientific approach that proved to be unaware of the physical basis for the first type of salience would be similarly unprepared for the second. Perhaps the best way of answering this question is to show that salience is also a significant factor in the attitudes of people toward the *objects* of ordinary experience and that it explains why the *scientist* and the *artist* differ so markedly in their views of objects. This expedient will enable us to contrast the typical characters of the scientific and the artistic approaches and to show that the more the scientist cultivates a scientific view of objects the more he disqualifies himself for aesthetic discussion.

An industrial engineer, for example, takes a highly specialized attitude to such a phenomenon as dust. To him, dust is a more rarefied form of an object, a kind of gas with the same explosive potential. An artist views dust with the mind of the multitude. Lack of moisture is now the important fact, and he and they express this in a simile, "dry as dust." To the scientist, one element among the properties of an object is not more important than any other. As a matter of fact, he exerts special care lest he overlook some minor property that might turn out to be more significant than the obvious ones. In contrast, the artist seizes upon the dryness of dust precisely because it expresses a perception that is available to everyone.

The artist, then, describes an object in terms of a dominant, universally recognizable component. This is another way of saying that he describes it in terms of a *salient characteristic*. The other components that figure in a scientific description are of little consequence to him. His faithfulness to reality lies in choosing the salient component and his unfaithfulness consists in ignoring the others. If his selection of the salience coincides with universal perception, the artist will consider it "true to life."

The artist has another purpose as well. He wishes to convey a sensation he is experiencing. He is referring to something that is "dry as dust" and of which he alone at the moment is aware. By comparing his own sensation with a universally granted perception, he obtains for it a similar recognition. Momentarily, an identity is established between a salience that everyone perceives and a salience that he alone perceives. "Their throats were as dry as summer dust" expresses a sensation in terms of a universal perception. The artist can perhaps venture "dry as the Sahara" or "bone-dry," but he cannot gain acceptance for "dry as a table," even though a table may be perfectly dry, because dryness is not the salient characteristic of "table."

While the artist's attitude does distort the object, it does not distort man's relation to objects because any resulting incongruity is the incongruity from one moment to all moments. His justification for describing the object in terms of its salient characteristic lies in choosing only one moment to do so. The scientist wants a description that remains valid for all moments. Yet there is a certain physical circumstance that sets a precedent for the artist's momentary description of objects: Consciousness itself cannot consider the object as a whole but only momentarily in single components or in small groups of them. The scientist is forced to compensate for this limitation upon consciousness by regarding each component of the object as the salient one from moment to moment. But his view is the specialized one of studying objects. Ordinarily, man recalls an object by its dominating component. Man is the layman, not the specialist, and this very lack of scientific objectivity or knowledge is at once a unifying influence on humanity and a boon to the artist. What may be imprecision or even ignorance to the scientist is also the accepted vocabulary of human experience.

The hazard in the scientific approach to the object arises during the attempt to reconstruct it from the momentary observations and measurements. Having avoided initial impressions of salience and having deliberately made each component of the object equally salient for the purposes of observation, the scientist must rearrange the object's components in some order of relative salience if he is to describe it as a whole object. The fault appears not when he selects some particular factor as a salient characteristic but when he attempts to relate this component to other components during his reconstruction of the entire activity.

It remains now to show how the performer's evocation of saliences among tones causes the shift in the listener's atten-

tion toward the context and reveals to him the salient characteristics of the passage. One of the best illustrations for this purpose is the performance of a song for voice and piano. We will
discuss a song by one of the great masters in this category,
Franz Schubert's setting of *Gretchen am Spinnrade*, from Goethe's
Faust.

Four components in the structure of its opening measures
have been labeled in Fig. 27 with numbers. Component I is the
bass, consisting mostly of dotted half notes but occasionally,

Fig. 27

Gretchen am Spinnrade, Op. 2, by Schubert

as in measure 4, adopting the rhythm of the tenor. Component II is the tenor, which keeps up a strongly iambic rhythm on the same pitch for lengthy periods of time. Component III, the alto, consists of a six-note figure in sixteenth notes that is repeated over and over. These three components constitute the piano part. The highest or soprano part, component IV, is the part for voice, which is made up of short phrases spaced by rests and couched in similar rhythm.

Although all music, in the interests of unity, tends to be repetitive from measure to measure, the four components that make up the structure of this song are repetitive to an unusual degree. The prevailing dotted halves of the bass, the constant iambic rhythm of the tenor, the incessant reiteration of the alto's figure, and the short, similar phrases in the soprano force us to the conclusion that Schubert wished a particular kind of monotony to be one of the song's essential features. The droning, reiterative effect of the opening measures is inescapable and the steady insistence of the four components is only intensified by continued emphasis upon the fifth of the chord.

At the same time, the continuity threatens to break away from this monotonous level to one that is charged with energy. The first such attempt comes in measure 7, which is marked by three features, strengthening of component II by additional notes, enlargement of the intervals in component III, and a sudden, disruptive shift in the harmony from a D minor to a C major chord. However, it is short-lived, and by measure 13 the monotony of the beginning has returned. In the course of the song, these outbursts become more and more sustained and reach strong climaxes. Since the monotonous and the energetic levels appear alternately throughout the song, Schubert has clearly desired the outbreak of energy to be another of its essential features.

The performers, then, first mark off the areas of the song that belong in each essential category. In Fig. 27, measures 1 through 6 constitute an area of monotony and measures 7 through 12 an area of outburst. The transition from the first to the second area is to be sudden, as the *crescendo* in measure 6 indicates, whereas the *decrescendo* in measure 11 signifies that the return is to take somewhat longer. The performers also notice that the composer has marked the first area *pianissimo* and the second area *forte*. Since these markings refer to import and not to specific intensities, they help remind the performers that soft tone is appropriate to monotony and loud tone to outburst of energy. The intention of the performers is to make the impression of monotony salient during the first six measures and to identify the impression of outbreaking energy with the remaining six.

The soprano can begin very softly because the voice gains

salience from contrast with the timbre of the piano. By locating the high points of nuance at the dotted quarter notes and by carefully observing the rests at the end of each phrase, she can bring out the similarity of the phrases and add their effect to the purpose of reiteration. At measure 7, where the second area begins, the timbre of her voice must take on increased richness, and she must reserve special salience for the first tone of measure 10, which is the climax of this still relatively restrained outburst.

The pianist, meanwhile, makes his contribution to the monotonous level of the first six measures by merging the tones as much as possible. He has the delicate task of making the fifth of the chord evident without upsetting the smoothness of the sixteenth-note figure. Since the three components of the piano part reinforce each other through coincidence of partials, notes in the figure could suddenly obtrude and make it seem disjointed. However, reinforcement also eases the problem of sustaining the bass, and the interjection of the bass eighth note in measure 4 is helped by its low register.

Commencing with measure 7, where the energetic area begins, the pianist weighs the effect of the added notes in the tenor against the need for increased intensity, and at the severe dissonance in measure 8, marked *forte*, estimates how much salience is conferred by the dissonance itself. He will no longer merge the sixteenth notes of the figure but increase their distinctness and rhythmic vitality. He also has the main responsibility for the sudden shift from the first to the second area and for the gradual return.

Although these are but a few of the requirements for the performance of Schubert's song, they serve to explain how the similar purposes of the components are detected and combined to form total impressions of salient characteristics and how saliences among tones are utilized to make those characteristics evident. As the similarity of purpose among the components changes with the course of the music, so the salient characteristics of the passages alter as well as the distributions of the saliences among the tones. Yet successive salient characteristics will remain related—in this instance, through alternation—since the music is planned for unity. Whenever they do not seem sufficiently related, the fault can be that of either the performer or the composer.

As the discussion of the Sarabande showed, the title of the music can point to the salient characteristics of passages but analysis of the structural components must substantiate their presence. Here, we have already reached many decisions about the performance of the song from such analysis and without referring as yet to Goethe's poem. But Schubert intended this song to be a setting of the poem and, for its bearing upon the performance, we must inquire into how we become convinced that he carried out his intention successfully. In the first stage, since the poem is based on human experience—it is spoken by one of the characters in a play—we apply criteria to it from our own experience. It is true that Gretchen can ruminate on her plight as she spins; she will be torn between her passion and her sense of sin; her thoughts will oscillate between the depths of despair and the exaltation of love. Confirming our detection of the two areas in Schubert's music, we become aware that the poet is also contrasting two states, Gretchen's former peace of mind and her present turmoil. "My peace has fled, my heart is sore," this phrase alternates with phrases of longing for Faust, "His hand's fond pressure and ah—his kiss!"

We thus perceive an identity of structure between the poem and the song. It is true that we perceive this identity more easily because the poem and the song are presented together and the states that are contrasted occur at the same moments. Yet what compels us to agree that the song sets the poem successfully is the similarity of the salient characteristics of the parallel passages in both. These perceptions on our part constitute a second stage in which we apply a new group of criteria to the composer's share of the presentation, drawing again on our own experience and checking our observations against the music itself. It is true that thoughts in rumination are fragmentary and interrupted. The human voice rises in pitch under agitation: the melody rises and falls with the intensity of the accompanying thoughts. Great intensity of emotion does build up over a period of time; the harmonies become more intense and the structure more complex with the buildup of agitation. Above all, we recognize that the composer has contrasted the salient characteristics of two types of passages that are appropriate to the salient characteristics of the two states that are contrasted in the poem. As these salient features of the context change from one passage to the other, we are convinced that they parallel the changes in the continuum of human experience to which both the poem and the music apply.

The third stage in our response to the song is the stage of performance, and here the tests we apply could take the form of questions. How would Gretchen voice the words, "My peace has fled, my heart is sore?" Would not the sensation of despair lead her to use low tones and nuances that die away in weakness? How intense should her tones become as she speaks more and more passionately of Faust's qualities? These questions are partly answered by our requiring of the singer the same tonal appropriateness that we would demand of the actress in Goethe's play.

As to the piano part, we ask, does the playing of the sixteenth-note figure create at the beginning an impression of droning, monotonous repetition and later reflect the increased intensity of expression? Has the pianist properly judged the effects of dissonance in the harmonies so that they are appropriate to the changing inflections of the voice? Does the piano part supplement the singer's expression or obtrude? Does it re-establish the initial character at every return to the opening measures? We wish to know whether the saliences among tones achieved by the performers support the criteria we have applied during the two preceding stages. Their success in meeting this requirement will be proportionate to the keenness of their observation of human characteristics and to the insight with which they have utilized universally granted features of human experience.

IV THE AESTHETICS OF PERFORMANCE

21 THE NATURAL SALIENCE OF MUSICAL MATERIALS

The aesthetics of performance begins with the basic paradox that has figured so largely in our discussion: No two interpretations of the same musical score are alike, and those above a certain level of competence are equally valid. Our ears attest this statement when, for example, we hear the same Chopin score interpreted by Alfred Cortot, Artur Rubinstein, Myra Hess, and others. The Schwann and Gramophone catalogues of recordings attest this statement by listing, for example, more than a dozen currently available performances of Beethoven's Fifth Symphony that differ from each other in many respects. Scientific investigation has gone further. Instead of depending on the ear, measuring instruments have been employed and have proved that at the same moment in the score the different performances used different duration and intensity values.

Thus, the hymn tune in Fig. 28 appears in conjunction with an experiment cited in Frank Howes's valuable book *The Borderland of Music and Psychology*.[38] (Below the tune, I have added a set of mathematical duration values that prevail when a quarter note equals ·90 of a second.) Four organists were asked to play the hymn, and meanwhile, by means of electric contacts attached to the keys, the duration values they employed were registered in hundredths of a second, Fig. 29. Howes does not discuss the implications of the experiment in detail, possibly because he was otherwise occupied with a main topic, the nature of rhythm.

However, the psychologist Carl E. Seashore, who devised tests for measuring musical talent, did give close attention to such differences in duration values from performer to performer. He developed his own methods of measuring them and, using these measurements as a basis, elaborated the *theory of deviation* to explain them. (It is still the prevailing theory among psychologists.) The performer, he said, first masters true pitch, even loudness, metronomic time, and pure tone, and then, using a kind of artistic license, *deviates* from them in order to

FIG. 28

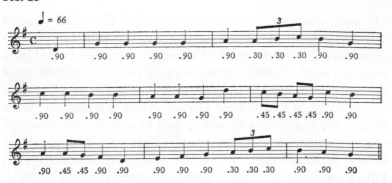

create beauty in his rendition. As far as "metronomic time" is concerned, for example, the performer would first master such mathematical duration values as those in Fig. 28 and then deviate, arriving at varied values like those of Fig. 29.

In his book *In Search of Beauty in Music*, Seashore enlarged the idea of artistic license to deviate into a system of aesthetics: "The reason for this musical license is that beauty in the rendition of a composer's design lies most frequently in the artistic play with deviations from the regular—true pitch, even loudness, metronomic time or pure tone or any of their combinations or derivatives. Here is a basic esthetic principle." [39] The verb "to deviate," which gives this theory its title, is of course intransitive and requires the preposition "from." The performer must be deviating from something, and, in Seashore's aesthetics, this "something" is the "regular."

As his use of the term "regular" indicates, Seashore is assuming the existence of an absolute in each of the four areas—pitch, duration, intensity, and timbre—from which the performer is free to deviate. This assumption requires a second one. Since the performer would have to master the "regular" before he could deviate from it, Seashore also assumes the

Fig. 29

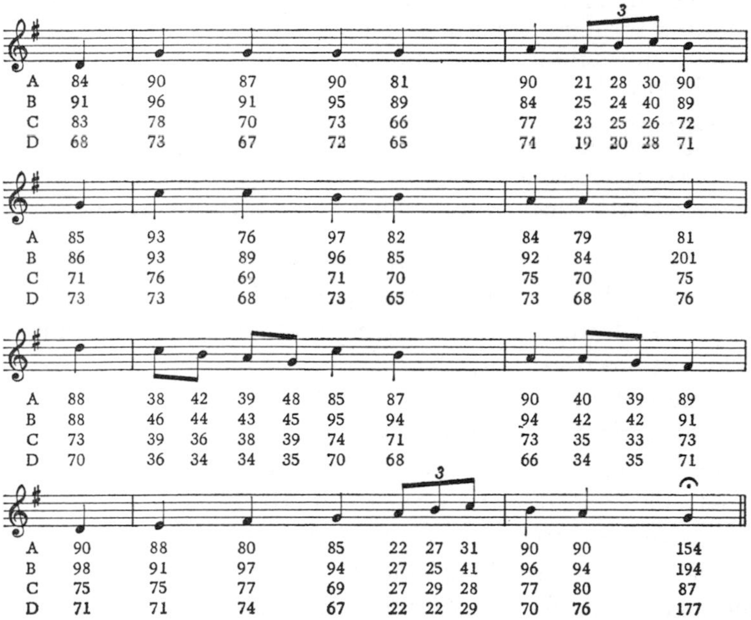

A	84	90	87	90	81		90	21	28	30	90
B	91	96	91	95	89		84	25	24	40	89
C	83	78	70	73	66		77	23	25	26	72
D	68	73	67	72	65		74	19	20	28	71

A	85	93	76	97	82	84	79	81
B	86	93	89	96	85	92	84	201
C	71	76	69	71	70	75	70	75
D	73	73	68	73	65	73	68	76

A	88	38	42	39	48	85	87	90	40	39	89
B	88	46	44	43	45	95	94	94	42	42	91
C	73	39	36	38	39	74	71	73	35	33	73
D	70	36	34	34	35	70	68	66	34	35	71

A	90	88	80	85	22	27	31	90	90	154
B	98	91	97	94	27	25	41	96	94	194
C	75	75	77	69	27	29	28	77	80	87
D	71	71	74	67	22	22	29	70	76	177

existence of a preliminary stage when the performer acquires the necessary mastery of the absolutes. Thus, he states: "The performer must be able to intone in true pitch and metronomic time with precision before he can master the skills of artistic deviation from them."[40] The risk in assuming a preliminary stage of mastery arises from the distinction it implies between highly skilled art and ordinary art, a distinction that is difficult to maintain and that leads to many contradictions. For example, the art of folksingers and other natural musicians is undeniable, and yet they do not undergo the type of training that Seashore envisages. Children, too, achieve artistic results, and modern musical education is based on the idea of encouraging them to reach expression at the earliest possible moment.

The theory of *deviation* widens its distinction between highly skilled and ordinary art in a further, doubtful way. It identifies deviation from musical absolutes with deviation from conventional standards of behaviour. Here, Seashore observes:

> Temperament shows itself in exceedingly fine responsiveness to tones which may be a matter of utter indifference or impossibility to the unmusical. This capacity is largely inborn both in the way of sensitivity to sound and a general nervous, if not neurotic, disposition, and is in itself enough to make the musician different from other people. Artistic license as a medium of self-expression is therefore, clear evidence of a musical temperament.[41]

The theory of deviation can draw scant support from this statement. Psychoanalysis has revealed the universality of "nervous" traits, and the amazing growth of amateur musical activities has testified to the universality of musical talent.

Finally, the theory of deviation has evidently confused the idea of musical absolutes with the image of the printed musical page. It is as if the performer finds these absolutes on the page before him and deviates from them. However, musical structures can be mastered directly, without the aid of the music page, and for a very long time they were. Untold centuries of musical history elapsed before the first primitive forms of notation came into existence, and many more centuries were required to develop it into its present form. Music was transmitted orally, and, as we have shown, present-day notation still presupposes an extensive oral supplement to the score. The music page simply enables the performer to comprehend the musical structure and offers nothing to be deviated from. The score only *seems* to be couched in terms of metronomic time, true pitch, even loudness and pure tone. "Metronomic," "true," "even," "pure"—these terms arise from an illusion and merely reflect the choice of musical material for a certain property that we shall call *natural salience* and now define and discuss.

By natural salience, we mean the extent to which nature has endowed the musical materials of the score with readily perceivable characteristics. We have dwelt on what the composer and performer do to further their purposes with salience. Now we must examine the musical materials that they have to work with and that their predecessors have selected from the phenomena of nature by a slow, infinitely detailed process over thousands of years. How much the composer and performer contribute and how much nature contributes will be difficult to decide and will vary with each instance. Yet the distinction is there as surely as sea and land and creatures existed before man appeared.

The octave, for example, is a natural phenomenon. Its discovery was probably a by-product of singing in unison, because it offers the nearest thing to duplication when male and female voices sing together. The octave is also the first upper partial of a musical tone and could have been detected through this circumstance. After the unison, it is the most pleasant-sounding interval, and the pleasure it gives disappears when it is perceptibly flatted or sharped. In short, nature has endowed the octave with a striking, characteristic harmoniousness and thereby given it a definite *advantage for salience*. This advantage not only led to the octave's discovery but made it the basis for music of all ages and countries.

Mankind has always been attracted to powers or qualities that are inherent in certain objects, and we should think of natural salience as implying an efficacy in musical materials that is analogous to the ascription of magical properties to objects. As one would expect, natural phenomena that affect the five senses to extreme degrees have attracted most attention and interest. These extremes of sensation may be said to have been "perceived" when they were associated with objects and located in ranges between opposites, as fire-hot, ice-cold; honey-sweet, gall-bitter; glitter-bright, rust-dull, etc.[42] We no longer attribute magical powers to objects that stimulate extreme sensations, but we still give such objects our special attention and interest. Primitive man took practical advantage of them for his magical purposes; we still regard them as having advantages for salience and conjure with them in art.

The same organization into ranges between extremes is evident in musical materials: high-low pitch, loud-soft intensity, long-short duration, and pure-mixed timbre. These ranges have also been subdivided in more or less mathematical ways. The range of pitch was divided into musical intervals by a very gradual process that subjected them to long, preliminary experimentation before they were finally accepted. The criterion for accepting them was their degree of consonance; and the grading of the intervals according to consonance, with the harmonious unison and octave at one extreme and the dissonant minor second at the other, is also the order in which they were accepted. Each acceptance was ultimately prompted by a natural advantage for salience, and, interestingly, it paralleled a progression from small to large numbers. The pitch ratio for the octave is $2 : 1$; for the fifth, $3 : 2$; for the fourth, $4 : 3$, etc.

By a similarly long and gradual process, the range of duration was divided into a series of note values, the duration of each note value being one half that of the next larger one in the series, as whole note, half note, quarter note, eighth note, etc. The criterion in this case was the fact that the ear can measure unequal durations most easily when one is twice or half as long as the other. By virtue of this natural peculiarity of hearing, time intervals that relate to each other as do numbers in a geometric series based on 2 acquired the natural salience that assured them a place in notation.

As to intensity, we have already seen that the range between minimum softness and maximum loudness was divided into another but approximate geometric series: *mezzo-forte*, *forte*, *fortissimo*, etc. Such subdivision of the range of intensity is not as valid as the subdivision of duration because the ear cannot tell that one intensity is double another. This limitation upon the ear is undoubtedly the reason why notation applies dynamic marks to portions of passages rather than to individual notes. One predominant level of intensity is to contrast with another, and therefore the listener is enabled to derive one general impression of intensity at a time without interference from the differences in salience within the passage.

In the case of timbre, too, we have already discussed the manner in which natural and synthetic timbres become useful to producing saliences among tones. Here, in keeping with the topic of subdivision of ranges, we may cite the classification of instruments into four types, string, woodwind, brass, and percussion, and then the division of the pitch range offered by each type of instrument according to size. Since the pitch intervals are repeated within each of the seven octave spans of the pitch range, the members of each type are turned into a family and the octave spans divided among them, as, violin, viola, 'cello, and double-bass. Such grouping into families must have been suggested by the repetition of intervals in the series of upper partials. It has the advantage of reducing an otherwise unwieldy pitch range to manageable proportions; it is important to orchestration for placing phrases in balanced contrast; it creates homogeneities of timbre that act like labels and identify individual components of the structure.

In all of the four categories of pitch, duration, intensity, and timbre, then, the composer and performer have at their disposal musical material that has already been selected for its advantages to salience. The effect of this selection in advance is to confer *universality* on musical materials, at least as far as Western music is concerned. The listener can be counted on to detect the various degrees of consonance of intervals, to recognize the distribution of note values within the beat, and to respond to contrasting intensity levels and contrasting tone colors. He becomes impressionable because musical material is derived from especially impressive phenomena of nature, because his auditory apparatus has been attuned in advance to the effects that are most likely to stimulate it.

Every performance, therefore, draws upon two sources of salience, the natural salience of the musical materials themselves and the structural saliences created by the composer and performer. The performer must judge how the composer has utilized natural properties to serve structural ends. When his judgment is faulty, the composer's combination of natural and structural salience is misrepresented. But when the performer's judgment is superior, he can actually enhance an inadequate composition by emphasizing the natural salience of its materials over its structural saliences. Here, we need a second term, *performance value*, to denote this exercise of judgment. Performance value refers to the performer's utilization of pitch, intensity, duration, and timbre in creating relationships of salience out of natural and structural conditions.

In view of the fact that the performer uses his individual judgment in his collaboration with the composer, it is a foregone conclusion that performance values will differ with different performers. Even when the composer's plan of saliences leans toward the extremes in each of the four ranges, performance values will inevitably differ because no two performers will sense and perceive to the same degree. This is the basic reason why the score stipulates the requisite kind of perception in relative terms and refrains from specifying the degree of intensity of perception that is to accompany it. The composer himself has no way of showing what attracted him to a particular salience because, once the goal of expression is reached in the score, the intensity of his experience has been taken up in the creation of the music itself.

The impression that a performer receives from the score, then, derives not from the intensity of experience that prompted the composer to write it but from the power of mind that embodied the saliences in it. By sensing the composer's creative power, the performer infers the intensity of the stimulus that led to the score. He then tries to match the composer's creativity with his own by searching in his own experience for a stimulus equal to the stimulus that went into the composition. For this matching of powers, the performer needs all the qualities and training we described in the synthesis of method. His effort will be similar to that of the composer in kind, but it will not be identical in degree. And both the kind and degree of perception he brings to bear will be reflected in his performance values for the musical score.

22   THE NATURAL SALIENCE OF NOTE VALUES

Where differences in performance values from performer to performer not only occur but are expected, one questions how much they can differ and still belong to the same score. As a helpful preliminary to discussing this question, we shall consider the same kind of problem in a more familiar area, namely, the judgment of time that self-developing film requires of the user. How did the inventor of this film decide upon a developing time of one minute? Clearly, he examined the resulting pictures after various intervals of time and concluded that the average time for a favorable outcome was one minute. For practical purposes, since no two individuals will peel off the negative at precisely the same moment, the inventor has in effect given a leeway of a few seconds before and after a minute of time. To borrow a term from measurement, he has permitted a *tolerance* of a few seconds. The film will develop in one minute plus or minus a few seconds.

This familiar situation brings out another point—that each user of the film must become aware of the inventor's criterion in selecting the wait of one minute. He must realize that a wait of, let us say, 58 seconds would result in a lighter picture and one of 62 seconds in a darker. At this juncture, too, further factors will enter, such as the conditions of lighting under which the picture was taken. As the number of factors multiply, it is evident that one photographer will *purposely* choose a developing time of perhaps 58 seconds and another a time of 62 seconds. The criterion for either of these choices will be the individual photographer's judgment of the effect on the resulting picture.

Meanwhile, the inventor is safe in setting a development time of one minute. He is safe because he has determined a *permissible range* or *tolerance* for the operation of the film. If the user's choice of developing time is between, let us say, 58 and 62 seconds, the inventor's criterion for a favorable outcome will [be satisfied. But he offers only generally favorable results. For a result that satisfies the individual user's criterion, for one that takes into account local, contributing factors, the choice of developing time must not only be within the established tolerance but meet the requirements of a particular picture.

Every specification of a tolerance depends on the physical nature of what is being measured and the use to which it is put. A farmer who wishes his plants to be spaced a foot apart will not be concerned if some of the seeds lie 11 or 13 inches apart. But a shaft may require machining to a tolerance of ·05 inch, that is, so that its diameter turns out to be within ·05 inch more or less than the specified measurement. It is significant that the determination of tolerances makes different demands on the persons who are to do the measuring. There will be more people who can sow seeds than can machine shafts. But as long as the requisite ability can be assumed, the existence of the tolerance will permit different individuals to arrive at different measurements and still meet the specification.

The possibility of a tolerance also presupposes a safe area for one act of measurement that does not interfere with the safe area for another. For example, a spacing of plants that assures them proper sunlight may not also provide them with sufficient nutrition. Or, a properly machined shaft may still give way under too great a stress. It is this necessity, this provision that the tolerances for similar acts of measurement not intrude on one another, that protects the specification from too wide a fluctuation of individual differences in measurement. The individual whose measurement falls outside the tolerance limits has in reality measured something else.

Keeping the circumstances of this preliminary discussion in mind, we can now explain how notation permits differences in performance values for the specifications contained in the same notation symbol. Since note values, for example, form a series in which the duration of one is twice the next, a tolerance is created for each. If a performance value falls within the tolerance for one note value, it represents that note value because it cannot represent the next in the series. In most instances, too, the exigencies of musical design act to reduce the number of different note values in any one passage, and the performer needs only to differentiate several consecutive note values of the series. It is an extremely rare musical passage that contains all the note values in the series from whole note to 128th note, including the single-dotted, double-dotted, and triple-dotted possibilities.

A simple illustration of this aspect of the tolerance will therefore be as acceptable as a complicated one, and we shall return to the hymn tune in Fig. 28, which contains only quarter notes, eighth notes, and eighth-note triplets. Setting the metronome at quarter note equals 66—that is, at 66 strokes to the minute—will allot roughly ·90 of a second to each quarter note. An eighth note will then have a duration of ·45 of a second and the eighth note of a triplet ·30 of a second. With a tolerance of plus or minus ·10 of a second, a performer could extend the duration of a quarter note to a second without creating confusion with a dotted quarter note, which would have an allotted duration of 1·35 seconds. Similarly, he could reduce the quarter note's duration to ·80 of a second without encroaching on the eighth note's ·45 of a second or even on the dotted eighth note, which would be allotted roughly ·67 of a second. It is evident that the tolerance or permissible range of fluctuation decreases proportionately with the number of different note values in the passage. But the more careful performer will not intrude on the tolerance for a possible note value even when it does not appear in the score.

Going on to Fig. 29, which gives the duration values used

by four organists when performing this hymn, we now see that the significance of these duration values does not lie either in comparing the values of one organist with those of another or in comparing them with the mathematical values in Fig. 28. To apply the principle of the tolerance, we must examine the performance values of each organist in themselves. We must find his *average duration value* for each note value, and this will tell us the tolerance he employed.

For example, organist A's average duration value for a quarter note was close to ·86 of a second. Since his longest duration value for this note was ·97 and his shortest ·80, he permitted himself a tolerance extending from plus ·11 to minus ·06 of a second. His average for the eighth note was ·41 with a tolerance from plus ·07 to minus ·03. (Comparatively, at ·86 of a second for a quarter, an eighth note would come to ·43.) His average for the eighth note of a triplet was ·26, the tolerance extending from plus ·04 to minus ·05. (Again, at ·86 of a second for a quarter note, the comparative value for a triplet's eighth would be about ·29.) Thus, organist A's performance values did not encroach on each other or on other possible note values except in the case of the first eighth note of the triplets, which was too close to a sixteenth note.

The tempo of organist A's performance was about 70 strokes to the minute. A tempo is established by the average duration time for the note values that create a beat. We are careful to use the plural, *note values*, because a performer, in 4/4 time, must relate his tempo not simply to the quarter note but also to the half measure and the whole measure. He must apply on a larger scale his customary method of subdividing a quarter of the measure into smaller note values and fitting them into the beat. The following table brings out clearly that each of the four organists, despite the subdivision of the quarter measure into eighths and triplets (measures 2, 5, 6, and 7), made the average duration of a half measure and a whole measure very close to twice and four times, respectively, that of a quarter note:

Average and Tolerance	Per Triplet-Eighth	Per Eighth	Per Quarter	Per Half measure	Per Whole measure
Organist A	·26 +·05 −·05	·41 +·07 −·02	·86 +·11 −·06	1·71 +·09 −·08	3·42 +·07 −·09
Organist B	·30 +·11 −·06	·43 +·03 −·01	·91 +·07 −·07	1·82 +·07 −·09	3·64 +·07 −·16
Organist C	·26 +·03 −·03	·36 +·03 −·03	·74 +·13 −·08	1·47 +·10 −·08	2·95 +·10 −·06
Organist D	·23 +·06 −·04	·34 +·02 −·00	·70 +·06 −·05	1·41 +·08 −·06	2·82 +·05 −·05

When eighth notes and triplet eighths occur in the same tune, the player is required to divide the quarter measure's duration into two and three parts respectively. He is forced to change from one mode of calculation to the other without disturbing the flow of the music, and he is therefore in danger of failing to adjust soon enough. The following table shows how each of the four organists adjusted to the triplets in measures 2 and 7. The top line gives the values in round numbers for triplet-eighths at the performer's average for a quarter note. The next line contains the values for two sixteenth notes and an eighth note which is one of the rhythmic patterns that might result from a failure to adjust properly to triplets. The third and fourth lines are the actual values allotted by each performer for the triplets in the two measures:

	Organist A	Organist B	Organist C	Organist D
Values for triplet-eighths	·29 ·29 ·29	·30 ·30 ·30	·25 ·25 ·25	·23 ·23 ·23
Values for two sixteenths and an eighth	·22 ·22 ·24	·23 ·23 ·46	·18 ·18 ·36	·17 ·17 ·34
Actual values in meas. 2	·21 ·28 ·30	·25 ·24 ·40	·23 ·25 ·26	·19 ·20 ·28
Actual values in meas. 7	·22 ·27 ·31	·27 ·25 ·41	·27 ·29 ·28	·22 ·22 ·29

From this table, it is evident that organist B approached dangerously to within the tolerances for two sixteenth notes and an eighth. However, we also notice that all four organists felt a need for salience in the third note of the triplets, which has importance as the seventh of the dominant chord, and allotted it relatively long duration. Organist B was probably not habitually faulty in playing triplets but exaggerated his response to this need for salience. He was not able to respond without encroaching on the neighboring tolerances, and yet he, as well as the other three organists, kept the total duration time for the triplets well within the tolerances that had been established for the quarter note.

When interpreted in this way, the experiment with the four organists illustrates the meaning of the tolerance: If a performance value falls within the tolerance, it *represents* the note value appearing in the score. Such performance values as ·83, ·78, ·70, ·73, ·66, ·77 of a second, which organist C allotted to six consecutive quarter notes, *all represented* a notated quarter note because they fell within the permissible range of plus ·13 to minus ·08 the average duration of ·74 of a second. Some of these various durations could be accidental or attributable to changes in muscular control, in much the same way as a free-hand straight line has not the precision of a ruled one. But most of them are definitely purposeful. The performer's choice within the tolerance enables him to accomplish aims beyond duration and having to do with pitch, intensity, and timbre. He can vary the note's relative salience because the listener accepts the greater or lesser duration the tolerance grants as representing the one note value.

As the values fluctuate within the tolerance, the listener accepts them as one note value because he is orientated by the *beat*: The average duration time of the beat establishes the tempo. We cannot emphasize too often that music is not simply a succession of duration values. Duration values are secondary to the beat of a tempo, and as long as their fluctuation is within the tolerance, the beat will not be disturbed. Should a performance value exceed the tolerance limits, the listener will feel either that the beat has become irregular or that a new note-value has been broached. For it is the beat that enables him to recognize the natural salience of note values arranged in a geometric series. Even an untrained listener is so sensitive to the beat that he can detect either an increase or a decrease in the average duration of a given note value and interpret it to signify a *ritardando* or an *accelerando*. He can also suspend the beat momentarily for the sake of a *fermata*, or hold, and then resume it without difficulty.

To summarize: Out of the indefinite extension of duration, the performer establishes and the listener recognizes an average duration for a given beat which constitutes the tempo. Due to the fact that one note value in the series has twice the duration of the next, a natural salience is created for the usually limited number of different note values that are employed in any one musical passage. This natural salience is traceable ultimately to the ear's ability to measure unequal durations most easily when they are multiples of the number 2. The listener will not notice the changes in duration values within the tolerance as such but will feel them as differences in salience that serve a large variety of purposes. This circumstance enables the performer to select duration values within the tolerance and to affect a note's salience variously without disturbing the listener's recognition of its average duration.

23 THE NATURAL SALIENCE OF DYNAMICS

Dynamics or intensity values are more difficult to discuss than duration values because nature has provided for the measurement of time and not for the measurement of intensity. While man did invent the clock, he was able to relate its movements to the orbits of the planets. No such reference frame for intensity exists in nature beyond the limits of audibility at one extreme and of deafening volume at the other. However, as if to compensate for the lack of measurement by nature, the ear is extremely sensitive to variations in intensity. It can not only detect minute differences but also establish levels of similar intensities. Notation takes advantage of both of these aural abilities in a great variety of ways of which accent signs, nuances, and dynamic marks are only the most obvious.

Again, as a preliminary to discussing the natural salience of dynamics, we shall cite a similar situation in a more familiar area, namely, the use of stress accents in ordinary English speech. The speaker gives salience to certain syllables of words, and, as he does so, we can discern two purposes that motivate him. First, he wishes to help the listener recognize the word. The requirements for word recognition are to be found in a pronouncing dictionary. They are defined with the aid of phonetic symbols and accent signs. Significantly, the phonetic symbols permit discrimination among similar sounds, but the accent signs give no clue to the degrees of accentuation.

How salient should the accented syllable be? The dictionary is silent on this point. In reality, the decision is left to the people of an area. They determine the degree of accent, and the number of persons involved in the decision and the size of the area they occupy are proportional to their cohesiveness as a group. Words are in constant use, are continually pronounced, and as a great number of individuals speak the same words, a level of salience for the accented syllables is ultimately established. The establishment of this level constitutes what might still be called a natural salience, even though in this instance environment has taken over nature's province. The pronunciation of any one individual follows a predetermined groove, since each person expects the accent. Here, we have a universal in the same sense that a listener's ear is attuned in advance to the properties of musical materials. The child who is learning to speak behaves toward the established accent as if it were a phenomenon of nature, and when he has learned to pronounce, his accent utilizes the natural salience that the syllables have acquired in his environment by universal agreement.

As long as the purpose of establishing a level of salience is to further word recognition, only a *medium degree* of salience will be required. There is no necessity for sharp accent when the object is to derive meanings that are stated in the dictionary. We shall term the medium degree of salience that furthers word recognition *prosaic salience*. Since prosaic salience is a group phenomenon and no two individuals within the group will accent to exactly the same degree, the establishment of a level for accented syllables also provides for a tolerance, a range within which individual values can vary and still meet the specified accent.

Yet, due to the nature of salience, we cannot speak of only one level; it requires the establishment of at least two. To become aware of accented syllables, there must also be a level for the unaccented ones. Salience means salience *from*; it is a judgment based on a comparison of two established levels. Consequently, when a person has accented properly for the purpose of prosaic salience and brought his value—we may certainly refer to it as his performance value—within the permissible range of the tolerance, he has in reality produced the proper disparity between two levels. This explanation provides for the circumstance that some people's voices are louder, by nature, than others. When prosaic salience remains the object, the listener will discount individual differences in tone of voice and concentrate his attention on the extent of disparity between the two levels that the speaker has established.

There will be occasions, too, when an individual's performance values fail to achieve the usual disparity between these two levels. If such occasions are few and far between, the listener will consider them accidental or due to errors in speech. However, if they occur consistently and the speaker and the listener belong to the same group, the listener will conclude that a second purpose, beyond that of word recognition of prosaic salience, is intended. As the speaker widens the disparity between the levels for accented and for unaccented syllables, his object is to convey some aspect of his own state or condition. To carry out this intention, he will require a high degree of salience, which we shall call *poetic salience*. Poetic salience, then, is the high degree of salience produced by widening the disparity between the levels for accented and unaccented syllables.

Returning after this preliminary to the natural salience of dynamics in music, we can at once draw a parallel between *word recognition* in speech and *phrase recognition* in musical performance. Every musical phrase requires a particular accentuation in order to be recognized. Its tones must be arranged in a hierarchy of relative salience in the same manner that speech accents some syllables more than others. The parallel between speech and musical performance is neither forced nor accidental. Music became an independent art only after a long association with words, and it still bears the unmistakable stamp of this origin. Setting a poem to music will bring out all the more the original musical features that were developed in parallel with those of speech, but they are always present in instrumental music as well.

The simplest, most familiar music can illustrate these points. In Fig. 30, the theme of Beethoven's Minuet in G major, (a), has been submitted to the technique of reduction, (b), by eliminating the sixteenths, which musical analysis considers subordinate to the other notes. In performance, the player treats the sixteenths as a speaker treats unaccented syllables. He confers salience on the tones in (b) by giving them a tonal level that contrasts with a tonal level for the sixteenth notes. The tonal level for (b) is analogous to that for the odd-numbered, accented syllables in such a line as W. S. Gilbert's "When the foeman bares his steel, Tarantara, Tarantara" and the one for the sixteenths in analogous to that for the even-numbered, unaccented syllables. For the purpose of phrase recognition, the disparity between the two tonal levels is moderate, producing the medium degree of salience that we have called prosaic.

Notation is as silent about the relative salience of its notes as the dictionary is about the extent of accent on syllables. Yet the player must know how to pronounce phrases just as the speaker must know how to pronounce words. He acquires this knowledge by listening to other performers, initially as a child or as a student. He develops what we earlier termed *conversance with idiom*, which may now be said to include familiarity with the musical accent that prevails in his environment. The players of an area establish particular features of musical accent for a theme by performing it or one like it frequently. Naturally, there must always be a first performance of a new theme for which no model yet exists. But new themes are made by rearranging long-used materials, and their performance simply requires adaptation of the familiar to changed conditions.

Fig. 30

(a)

(b)

Whoever premières a new theme establishes tonal levels on the basis of his previous performance knowledge, and subsequent performances will either uphold his choices or establish others.

The established pronunciation for musical phrases, then, rests upon creation of levels of salience, so that notes of prior structural importance can be discriminated from subordinate ones. The effect of the disparity between these levels is to create a natural salience of dynamics. That is, the performer profits by a universal predisposition. Although he is the actual producer of levels, he does so in conformity with the prevailing pronunciation of musical phrases. He works in terms of the listener's expectation that a musical phrase will be accented in the prevailing way. If he accented the sixteenths in Fig. 30 instead of the dotted eighths, the listener would consider the theme mispronounced. The reaction would be the same as the reaction to accenting the even-numbered syllables in Gilbert's line.

Since the performers of an area prescribe the disparity between levels which makes for a natural salience of dynamics, a tolerance for permissible variations by individual players must necessarily exist. A player could vary the disparity within certain limits and still meet the specifications of the prevailing pronunciation. Yet he is also as free as a speaker is to widen it for the purpose of poetic salience. If he does this consistently, he has moved beyond aiding recognition of the phrase into a realm of personal interpretation. By employing a high degree of salience, he signifies his desire to convey an aspect of his own state or condition. However, he must remain true to the requirements for recognizing the phrase and must do nothing that would upset the hierarchy of salience among its tones. Giving greatest salience to the sixteenth notes in Fig. 30 would not come under the heading of poetic salience. It would still constitute mispronunciation. Since poetic salience is detected by comparison with prosaic, the two must be mutually reconcilable.

Throughout this discussion of dynamics, we have emphasized the term *salience* over the term *intensity*. Our emphasis has been an outgrowth of the previous chapter on the transformation of physical factors in performance. There, we brought out that the performer is vitally concerned with how much a tone stands out from or blends with other tones. As he compares them on the basis of their relative salience, he often finds that, due to local conditions, a tone played with less force of touch than another will turn out to be the more salient. Stated in another way, the performer cannot count on a constant correlation between force of touch and salience. Greater force of touch produces greater amplitude of string vibration, which, by definition, signifies greater intensity. But due to the local conditions of pitch location, reinforcement, state of dissonance, etc., greater force of touch does not necessarily produce greater salience.

To obtain contrasting tonal levels for structurally prior and subordinate notes, therefore, the performer cannot simply assign greater force of touch to the first group and less to the second. He must use a variety of means in which all four factors, duration, timbre, pitch, and intensity, figure to varying extents. The tones in the two groups *must seem to the listener* to belong to contrasting tonal levels, and, as the player performs successive or simultaneous tones, he makes each one seem to belong to the proper level by adjusting its degree of salience accordingly. One note will receive its proper salience through reinforcement, the next as a result of its dissonant state, a third from its position in the chord, etc. Each of these saliences will be evoked by some force of touch, but it will be a case of force plus the local conditions for salience and not a case of force that correlates with intensity.

For these reasons, the production of contrasting tonal levels takes on an experimental character. The absence of correlation between force of touch and salience, the constantly varying conditions for salience, and the need to make salience apparent to the listener rule out the possibility of a hard and fast approach, and the performer must adopt an attitude of judgment among many trials. The relative nature of disparity itself will help him considerably, but his situation is different from the purely mechanical ones of turning the knob on an amplifier or of enlarging a photograph or of changing the scale of a map. For, changes in the intensity of tone will bring about changes in tone color and in mutual reinforcement, and their effects upon salience can be separated out and predicted only after numerous trials and careful, discriminating listening.

One of the best illustrations of this need for an experimental attitude is the "echo effect," which requires the same passage to be first played *forte* and then *piano*. To explain how such an effect is possible, we must assume that the echo is not exact but sufficiently similar. We do know that the pianist can duplicate any one passage very closely. There is such a thing as a memory for forces of touch themselves, which is based on the muscular relations among them and acquired by constant repetition or practice. Accordingly, it is possible to reduce the total muscular energy while still retaining the relationships, as we do with common muscular tasks like hammering a nail less strongly or turning a faucet less vigorously. The musical result is not an exact echo because the conditions for salience have changed. But with minor adjustments for such changes and since the passage has already been heard, the effect of playing it with proportionately reduced energy is that of a recall, and the similarities between the two performances outweigh the differences.

Similarly, to endow a passage with *forte* dynamics, the performer begins with a generally strong force of touch and notices its effect on the conditions of salience. If this touch creates the levels for prosaic and poetic salience that he desires, he will retain it and commit to memory the muscular sensations that accompany it. After many such experiences, he will come to associate a range of touches with the dynamic mark *forte*, and tend to employ them for passages so marked. However, the relation between dynamic marks and forces of touch can never be direct or invariable. *Forte* in Mozart's music and *forte* in Beethoven's by no means signify the same range of dynamics. Indeed, the range is different from composition to composition of each of these composers. The number of tones in a passage, their relative dissonance, their location in registers and distribution in the pitch range, and many other considerations act to prevent correlation between dynamic marks and forces of touch. Here again, the passage must *seem to be forte* to the listener.

24 THE NATURAL SALIENCE OF THE PITCH INTERVALS

We have said that music selects from the range of pitch certain relationships that afford salient characteristics. These characteristics emerge during two phases of perception: (1) when the pitch distance or interval between any two tones is detected, and (2) when the degree of consonance that they create is estimated. Phase (1) is governed by the fact that pitch relationships in music form a scale bounded by an octave. Since each note of the scale is related to the first one, or keynote, the progress of a melody is often expressed as "departure" from the keynote with eventual "return" there to end or give an impression of finality. Also, since a melody is free to present the scale notes in any order, each of its tones is related not only to the keynote but to all the others, especially those immediately preceding and following. Inherent in the detection of a pitch interval is simultaneous relation to the keynote and the other notes of the scale; and the ability of tones to give off such relation *while the melody is in progress* constitutes a natural salience of pitch characteristics that is vitally important to musical structure.

In phase (2), the degree of consonance of any two tones is estimated. Besides rearranging the order of the notes of the scale, a melody places them in small groups or *motifs*, which, in turn, form larger groups or *phrases*. In order to comprehend a motif, the listener learns to keep each succeeding tone in mind until all of them have appeared. His listening activity thus extends over a period of time during which the state of consonance that exists among the motif's tones can become evident to him. This state of consonance will not be judged purely in terms of sensation. Instead, it will be related to a pre-existing system of chords that have been constructed on the basis of the scale and that again constitute a natural salience through universal acceptance. As each note of the scale relates to the keynote, so the chord built upon it relates to the keynote chord or tonic, and the consonant effect of any one chord will again depend upon a relation to the tonic and to the chords that precede and follow it in the progression. Harmonizing a motif means identifying its salient effect of consonance with one of the chords built on the scale. When a second motif appears in the phrase and creates a different effect of consonance, this new effect will be identified with another chord and the harmony will be said to change. From this harmonic point of view, the notes contributing to the effect of consonance are given a prior status in the musical structure and the remaining tones are considered subordinate to them.

Phase (1), or detection of the pitch interval, may then be termed the melodic phase of perceiving pitch relationship, and phase (2), or estimation of the degree of consonance, the harmonic phase. It is evident that the conditions for salience that exist during both of these phases will vary with the degree of proximity of the tones in time. In general, close temporal proximity of tones promotes harmonic perception whereas spaced occurrence of tones aids melodic perception. To some extent, the period of attentive listening, during which the hearer awaits completion of the motifs, will tend to modify the physical effect of different degrees of proximity. That is, to take in an entire phrase, he must correlate later appearing tones with earlier ones and must postpone conclusions until all have made their entrances. Nevertheless, the performer uses the physical conditions of proximity to great advantage.

One of the ways in which the player takes advantage of proximity is through the device called *legato*. *Legato* is accomplished on the pianoforte by delaying the cessation of one tone beyond the entrance of the next. The degree of *legato* is proportional to the extent of this delay. It is true that the greater the degree of *legato*, the longer the time the listener has to detect salient characteristics of a pitch relationship. Yet this grant of additional time to the hearer is not the purpose of *legato*. Its purpose is rather to direct his attention to melodic, harmonic, or rhythmic salient characteristics, depending upon the three possible types of proximity.

The first type of proximity is adjacent: when one tone ceases immediately upon the entrance of the next. They do become connected but only because there is no interval of silence between them. The connection is purely contiguous, permitting each tone to be heard as a separate entity, and, therefore, this type of proximity promotes the melodic phase of pitch perception. The second type of proximity is overlapping: when the cessation of one tone is delayed beyond the entrance of the next. Now they are connected differently because they are heard sounding together. They are briefly fused and each, temporarily, loses its individual identity. Thus, this second type of proximity aids the harmonic phase of pitch perception. The term *legato* refers to this type, whereas the first type or proximity through contiguity is designated by the term *non legato*. A third term, *staccato*, is applied to the third possible type of proximity, disparate proximity, or when one tone ends before the entrance of the next. *Staccato* creates an interval of silence between tones and therefore helps neither the melodic nor harmonic phases of pitch perception. By emphasizing the moments of entrance of successive tones, it serves rhythmic objectives.

The reader can verify these conclusions by a simple experiment. First, play a tone and its octave simultaneously. A harmonious impression results in which the two tones seem to merge into one total. Next, play the tone and follow it with its octave, taking care not to hold the first tone beyond the entrance of the second. The two tones are now distinct, and the impression of their harmoniousness is considerably reduced. Instead, the rise in pitch or melodic factor becomes very noticeable. Finally, play the tone and after it its octave, but hold the first tone beyond the entrance of the second before letting its damper fall. Now there is a momentary impression of harmoniousness before the rise in pitch is perceived. *Legato* has brought out the harmonic characteristics of the pitch relationship and added them to the melodic. To test the effect of *staccato*, silence the tone before the entrance of its octave. The entrances of each will be emphasized, adding a rhythmic impression to the perception of the pitch relationship.

Notation also has ways of indicating the three types of proximity without using the three terms. When the composer desires one note to cease with the entrance of the next, he notates only the notes themselves. When he wishes *legato* connection, he groups notes under a curved line. And when tones are to be separated by a silence, he places a dot or dash over the notes or a rest between them. It is obvious that the curved line does not indicate the extent of *legato*, nor does the *staccato* dot specify the length of the silence (the dash is understood to shorten the silence somewhat). Performers, then, will differ in their response to these indications. But all of them benefit from the enormous resources in these three ways of qualifying pitch perception. By varying the proximity of the tones in the relationships, they can make melodic or harmonic or rhythmic characteristics salient and influence the connotation of the listener's perception of pitch.

There is still a fourth way of notating proximity in time, namely, by means of the symbols for simultaneity. When a composer wishes notes to be played simultaneously, he either joins their heads by a single stem or places one vertically above the other with individual stems. In this term, *simultaneity*, we again encounter the concept of infinity that we cited in the discussion of measurement and the tolerance (Section 22). The effect of the concept of infinity is to make simultaneity a relative instead of absolute term. Whether two tones were played together will depend upon the precision of the measuring instrument. For example, on a tape recorder, tones that appear to be simultaneous at 7·5 inches per second are seen to be asynchronized at 3·75. We must therefore substitute the term *asynchronization* for simultaneity and refer to tones played together as asynchronized to varying degrees. Once more, too, the concept of a tolerance is needed in conjunction with the meaning of asynchronization. Here, the tolerance signifies that the length of time between the entries of tones notated to be played simultaneously will be the performer's average time plus or minus a number of hundredths of a second.

To illustrate this application of the tolerance, let us suppose that a performer played ten consecutive two-note chords, such as so-called double-thirds, which were notated in the score to be played simultaneously. The time intervals between the entries of the tones in each chord could have been respectively, in hundredths of a second: 1·7, 2·5, 3·1, 2·9, 1·2, 3·8, 2·6, 1·8, 3·5, and 2·1. The performer's average asynchronization, then, was 2·52 hundredths of a second. Since his greatest degree of asynchronization was 3·8 and his smallest 1·2, his tolerance was plus 1·28 and minus 1·32 hundredths of a second.

Although asynchronization of chordal tones may be due to lack of muscular control or to carelessness, there can be no doubt that in a majority of instances it is intentional. The performer treats the notation of simultaneity as a specification that is met by all the time intervals within the tolerance, such as the variety above. As each time interval falls within the limits of the tolerance, it signifies some intention of the player that will become evident to the listener as a result of the asynchronization. While all the performer's choices within the tolerance will seem to the listener to be instances of simultaneity, he will also be affected by attendant considerations of harmonic, melodic, and rhythmic nature.

Since chords, by definition, belong in the harmonic category, whatever the performer accomplishes through asynchronization will be above and beyond a primarily harmonic effect. Limited, then, by a primary harmonic purpose, the principles governing asynchronization are as follows: (1) the smaller the degree of asynchronization, the greater the salience of harmonic characteristics; (2) the greater the degree of asynchronization, the greater the salience of melodic characteristics; and (3) if the degree of asynchronization is greater than the duration of the chordal tones, rhythmic characteristics will become salient.

In Fig. 31, performance according to these three principles is represented graphically. The horizontal lines represent the tones of such four-note chords as the triad plus the octave above the fundamental and their inversions. The beginning of a line is the moment at which the tone enters; the length of the line is the tone's duration; extension of one line beyond the beginning of another means that both are heard together; the slant made by the beginnings of the lines represents the staggered entries of the tones; and the bracket above indicates the degree to which the tones are asynchronized. At (a) are various types of staggered entry. The degree of asynchronization is small, showing that harmonic salience is desired. Additional types of entry are illustrated at (b), but here the degree of asynchronization is larger, pointing to a melodic purpose in the performance. In the case of the varieties at (c), the duration of the chordal tones is less than the degree of asynchronization. As a result, rhythmic characteristics become salient.

Like the performer, the listener regards examples such as those in Fig. 31 as simultaneously played chords, and he does

FIG. 31

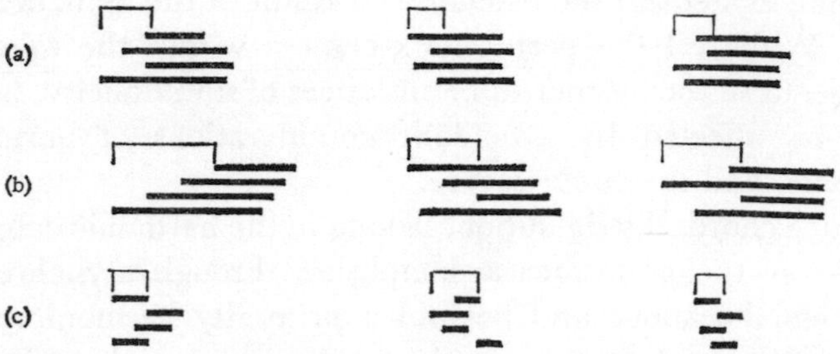

so not because he is incapable of detecting the asynchronization. L. N. Vernon, in his article "Synchronization of Chords in Artistic Piano Music," [43] states that most listeners can detect the asynchronization when two tones are played as little as ·02 of a second apart. Notwithstanding this capacity, it is essential that the listener remain oblivious of the asynchronization. He is not to notice the asynchronization but to derive its purpose. In order to submit to the effect of the harmonic, melodic, or rhythmic characteristics that become salient as a result of the asynchronization, he is to take for granted that a chord was played. For listeners have the capacity not only to detect asynchronization but to ignore it; they can establish a tolerance of their own for asynchronization. A striking instance of their adaptability in this respect is offered by performance on the harp. The characteristic breakage of chords while playing this instrument—the term *arpeggiation* comes from the Italian *arpeggiare,* which means "to play upon the harp"—is at first very apparent, but its effect soon wears off and the arpeggiated chords are accepted as simultaneously played. The hearers have established a tolerance for an unusually wide range of permissible fluctuations in asynchronization.

The harp, then, is an extreme instance, and ordinarily asynchronization takes place within much more minute intervals of time. For this reason, beyond referring in general, as we have done, to harmonic, melodic, or rhythmic objectives, it would at first seem futile to try and find out precisely what the performer's purposes are with his immensely varied types and

FIG. 32
Measures 23–25, first movement, Piano Sonata in F major, K.332, by Mozart

degrees of asynchronization. However, a highly significant circumstance intervenes to make this attempt much easier and more promising. In notation, *the composer practices asynchronization* on a larger scale in exactly the same way as the performer does on a smaller scale. Fig. 32 quotes measures 23, 24, and 25 of Mozart's Piano Sonata in F major, K.332, which illustrate certain types of asynchronization employed by composers. In the treble staff of measure 25, the diminished-seventh chord is stated by three notes in small type and one in large. Since the note values in large type already add up to the three quarters permitted by the time signature, the decisions about the duration values of the three miniature notes have clearly been left to the performer. He is to asynchronize the diminished-seventh chord in an appropriate manner.

His problem centers around two possible locations for the C-sharp and the B-flat: (1) whether the three miniature notes belong in the last eighth note of measure 24, or (2) whether they should be part of the first eighth of measure 25. A decision in favor of (1) would place the B-flat at the beginning of measure 25; one in favor of (2) would place the C-sharp there. Most performers choose (1) because beginning measure 25 with the B-flat is more desirable melodically, that is, by providing a high, accented point to the phrase. They asynchronize the chord commencing with the latter portion of the last eighth note in measure 24 and ending on the downbeat of measure 25. Individual performers will differ more in locating the point during the last eighth note where the asynchronization should begin than in deciding the precise moment on the downbeat when it should end. Those who favor a stronger accent on the high B-flat will start the asynchronization later during the last eighth note of measure 24. The resulting decrease in the degree of asynchronization sharpens the accent.

Another typical form of asynchronization appears in this example from Mozart in the bass staff. Employing numbers to represent the height of pitch in the chord, the bass figures in measures 23 and 24 follow the order 135353. Such figures also come under the heading of broken chords, but, unlike the instance of the diminished-seventh chord, the sum of their notes is dictated by the time signature. Since their melodic outline is of little importance, the degree of asynchronization in performing them will vary according to whether the player considers their harmonic or their rhythmic significance the more appropriate to the passage. The propriety in terming these basses examples of asynchronization, therefore, consists not in their notation but in the harmonic or rhythmic objectives they serve. Thus, the sixteenth notes in measure 23 and the eighths in the treble of measure 24 are not instances of asynchronization, because, although they, too, are broken chords, they serve melodic, not harmonic or rhythmic, purposes.

Does a composer mean something different by notating miniature notes instead of the wavy line of arpeggiation? This question is not easily answered. Possibly, the wavy line is a symbol of a lesser degree of asynchronization or of harmonic or rhythmic objectives, and the notes are written out when he wishes their melodic contour to be emphasized. (The problem, of course, concerns only upward arpeggiation, because a composer is forced to use miniature notes for downward arpeggiation, the baroque sign that indicated it having long since been out of use.) In the form of asynchronization peculiar to Chopin's music, the miniature notes and the wavy line mean the same thing. Whether Chopin notates (a) or (b) in Fig. 33, both signify (b). Such use of alternative symbols is consistent

Fig. 33

with the improvisatory aspect of Chopin's melodic writing and with the unusually large share of the collaboration that he asks the performer to assume.

In Fig. 31 above, we gave various examples in which the performer produced asynchronization by staggering the entry of chordal notes. All of these, on a larger scale, and many more have been actually notated by composers. Changing the mode of representation, therefore, from horizontal lines to the initial letters of the four vocal parts, *S*oprano, *A*lto, *T*enor, and *B*ass, some of the ways of creating permutations are as follows: (1) altering the order of occurrence, as S—A—T—B, B—T—A—S, S—T—A—B, A—S—T—B, etc.; (2) sounding two or three of the tones simultaneously, as

$$\begin{array}{ccc} \text{S—T} & \text{S—A} & \text{S} & \text{A} \\ & & \text{A—B,} & \text{T—S, etc.} \\ \text{A—B,} & \text{B—T,} & \text{T} & \text{B} \end{array}$$

(3) assigning different permutations to each of the hands and playing them together. In Fig. 34 are several examples of asynchronization by Debussy, who was particularly ingenious in devising new permutations. Some of these remind us of the

FIG. 34
Passage from Etude XI, by Debussy

problems of the small hand in playing chords with a large spread. Players with small hand-spans are forced to asynchronize large chords, but they develop sufficient skill to bring the degree of asynchronization within a tolerance, and then the listener accepts the chords as simultaneously played. Examples from Chopin in Fig. 35 illustrate both the device of playing two notes with the thumb (in this case, black keys, too) and the necessity, even for large hands, to leap during asynchronizations that cover a wide pitch area.

The composer, then, has provided the models for the performer's activity with asynchronization. Whatever the composer gains from asynchronization on a larger scale will be repeated by the performer on a smaller scale and with the same

FIG. 35
Prelude Op. 28, No. 7, by Chopin

Etude Op. 25, No. 5, by Chopin

devices. We must inquire into the composer's methods and devices, therefore, if we would understand the performer's behavior with asynchronization, and our starting point for such an inquiry is in a realization about the nature of chords themselves. *Chords are incidental to voice-leading.* A chord is a vertical cross-section of the horizontal motion of vocal parts. It has no primary status in musical structure but obtains a secondary one through analysis. The act of cross-sectioning creates a chord in much the same way that annual rings appear when a tree is cut down: the ring is an analyzed circumference from what in reality is cylindrical. Consequently, each note in one of the permutations of asynchronization has a contrapuntal role primarily and a harmonic role only secondarily.

FIG. 36

Molto allegro e vivace, Piano Concerto No. 1 in G minor, Op. 25, by Mendelssohn

These two roles are illustrated by Fig. 36, a pattern of asynchronization from the last movement of Mendelssohn's Piano Concerto in G Minor, Op. 25. At (a), its four component parts have been scored as they would be played by four violins or flutes. At (b), they have been formed into chords. Fig 36(c) shows their order of asynchronization to be A—S—T—B. Since the pattern does not change from chord to chord, the notes belonging to each vocal part occur at the same position in the order of succession. This adherence to one order enables the ear to follow the motion of the vocal parts despite the asynchronization.

In deciding which of the four parts carries the main theme, we at once rule out the tenor and bass as melodically deficient due to repetitiveness. The alto and soprano have equal claims but the decision goes to the soprano through what we have called salience as a result of position. The topmost tones have the main melody, and, accordingly, the ear must wait until the second tone of the pattern of asynchronization appears in order to derive the theme. The first note of such patterns usually carry the theme because its location at the beginning of a beat makes it more salient. The effect Mendelssohn gains, therefore, arises from assigning the important responsibility of carrying the theme to notes that are in a less important rhythmic location. In reality, he has syncopated the theme, that is, accented weaker rhythmic locations more than stronger. The theme becomes livelier, more whimsical, and more amusing. It takes on one type of characteristics that result from syncopation, in much the manner of Fig. 36(d).

On a smaller scale, the performer achieves similar results with his asynchronizations. He, too, can affect a tone's salience by relating its location in the order of asynchronization to its role of carrying a vocal part. In the two measures of Field's Nocturne No. 4 in A major, Fig. 37, the composer has called for asynchronization of the treble chord. The last three eighth notes in the treble staff of the first measure have the function of an anacrusis or lead-in to the reappearance of the melody in the second measure. Thus, the soprano A at the beginning of the second measure is at once the outcome of the anacrusis and the restart of the theme. To fulfill this double significance is the purpose of the asynchronization. The three eighth notes of the anacrusis have set up an expectation of when the A is to appear. The asynchronization, by delaying the arrival of the A until after the two miniature notes are heard, at once heightens that arrival and announces the resumption of the theme. The A has been given greater salience, thereby calling attention to its double melodic function.

We may say, therefore, that asynchronization of chords by the performer is a device to give salience to the changing purpose of the voice-leading by which they are governed. At this

FIG. 37
Measures 4 and 5, Nocturne No. 4 in A major, by Field

point, however, we shall not draw further parallels between the composer's and the performer's aims with asynchronization because they are treated in detail in the next chapter. For the same reason, we shall also postpone additional details of the natural salience of tone color and go on to a consideration of certain innate abilities.

25 INNATE RESPONSES TO NATURAL SALIENCE

The performer's ability to duplicate a passage very closely each time he plays it presupposes a power to create closely similar duration values at will. However remarkable this power may seem to us, it is not confined to a few gifted individuals but possessed by everyone. Each person has the innate capacity to achieve the closely similar durations that fall within the tolerance for a given note value. The universality of a capacity that requires such fine discrimination seems at first surprising, but basically it is an activity of comparison and the individual no more needs a metronome to compare durations than he needs a ruler to know whether one line is longer than another. The ear has the same ability to judge time intervals as the eye has for space distances.

We can therefore expect the innate capacity to create similar durations to be manifested in many familiar ways. For example, at a baseball game, the fans often clap in unison to rally the team. There can be no doubt that the clapping is started by one person. He sets the tempo and the others join in. How does he begin? Either at random or by choice, he creates a time interval with his first and second claps, which he then duplicates with a third clap, a fourth, a fifth, etc. His method is that of addition. He adds each time interval to the preceding one. By means of an innate judgment or sense of time, he compares the coming interval with the one that has just transpired and achieves their close similarity. They are not exactly alike but vary within a small enough tolerance to be accepted as exactly alike.

Next, a second fan hears the first one's clapping and joins in. To do so, he judges the first fan's time intervals by comparing several consecutive durations. His method, at the outset, is to match his time intervals to those of the first fan. But soon he is launched on his own and adds each succeeding time interval to a preceding one that he himself has created. Two instances of tolerances are involved in this transition from imitation to autonomy: The second fan's time intervals will not be exactly like those of the first but will fall within the permissible range of fluctuation that the first has set; also, when he comes to create his own time intervals, they will not be exactly alike and will themselves vary within a certain tolerance. However, both the imitative and the autonomous tolerances must match sufficiently for it to be said that the two fans have clapped in unison. As more of the spectators join in and this process is repeated by each, the remarkable thing is that they all keep the tolerances sufficiently narrow in range to maintain the first fan's original tempo.

When evaluating such abilities to keep time, one can easily fall into the trap of regarding the clap as more significant than the time interval. Since the clap marks the end of the time interval, one tends, then, erroneously to measure the duration of the interval by the clap. A clap and a duration are two completely different things and must not be confused. Duration is time, and the sensation that time has elapsed depends on experience. A time interval is not expressed by a marker at its end but by what transpires during it. For this reason, there is a fundamental association between duration and movement, which is exemplified by the movements of the conductor's baton. These movements of the baton are the analogues for the musical experience that transpires during time intervals. In a very real sense, the baseball fans are not clapping their hands in unison but moving their arms in unison.

It is this association between time intervals and movement that enables the performer to achieve *purposely* different durations within the tolerance and then to remember them. The fact that he is in action during the time interval gives real existence to what, in the form of judgment, can only be imagined. He can take a longer or shorter time to do something. He can stretch or contract a time interval by correlating the motions for a particular task with their durations. As he compares time interval B with time interval A, C with B, D with C, etc., he fixes each one in his mind by associating with it his own movements during the time as well as those of the instrument. For example, since keeping the key depressed with his finger prevents the damper from falling and silencing the strings, he will relate the release of the key to the upward motion of his finger. Interval A was produced by such and such an upward motion, interval B by such and such, etc. The association of muscular motion with tonal duration means engaging simultaneously in two categories of comparison: comparing successive durations and comparing successive motions. Interval B was shorter than A as a result of motion X; interval C was longer than B as a result of motion Y, etc. After much practice, the performer learns to reproduce these comparative relations between successive durations and successive motions, and when he has learned to do so, it is said that he purposely achieved the different durations. Since each rendition is a new actuality and requires physical effort, the listener gets the impression that the performer is intentionally producing time intervals when he is really reproducing muscular motions that he has learned through practice.

Throughout this process, the performer's method with duration remains additive. He adds interval B to interval A as he compares the two. However, within his procedure by addition, he also subdivides. The addition comes first and produces time intervals that are accepted as equal because they fall within the tolerance. Thereafter, as we saw in Fig. 29, the experiment with the four organists, these intervals may be subdivided for the purposes of the smaller ones that they comprise. Organist B, for example, maintained an average duration per quarter measure, half measure, and whole measure of ·91, 1·82, and 3·64 seconds respectively, despite his greater freedom with the eighth notes. The same correlation by the other three—A's ·86–1·71–3·42, C's ·74–1·47–2·95, and D's ·70–1·41–2·82— points to the generally accepted fact that performers, in 4/4 time, can *think* in whole and half notes as well as in quarters. When it comes to playing eighth notes and triplet-eighths, therefore, they achieve the subdivision by re-engaging in addition on the smaller scale, that is, by comparing the eighths with one another within the limits set by the supravening quarter note. The choice of durations for the eighth notes will vary with their structural functions, but the tolerance they observe will have to be correlated with the ones for the larger note values. From eighth note to eighth note, the attitude is additive, but the need to relate their tolerance to the prior ones for the quarter measure, half measure, and whole measure turns the process into a subdivision.

This insistence on the primacy of the additive method follows from the *successive* nature of time intervals in music. The time intervals must be successive because the act of comparing them is also the act of creating them. We ordinarily call this situation *rhythm* and the highly characteristic sensation that accompanies it *the sense of rhythm*. We speak of a sense of rhythm because of the strong factor of *participation* that is involved. Participation is the human impetus on which the successive, additive nature of the time intervals depends. The closely similar time intervals cannot "get going" and be "kept going" until, like links of a chain—or more dynamically, like vibrations of a string—they form an uninterrupted succession; and it is the pulse of constantly maintained acts of comparison which guarantees that succession against interruption.

Any interruption in the stream of successive comparisons, therefore, will break the chain of successive time intervals. Interval C compares with interval A because C compares with B and B with A. There is no reference to an outside standard. Any "standard" is merely the possibility of obtaining, by objective investigation, an average duration for the closely similar time intervals. Such averages are purely scientific and depend on measuring the intervals after they have been created. The performer himself is completely unconscious of an average time interval. He is conscious only of participating in acts of comparison that create closely similar, successive time intervals and that convince him the intervals are alike.

We have taken great pains to emphasize this absence of an outside standard for the performer's acts of comparison because it pinpoints the basic difference between the tolerance theory and the deviation theory. The idea of deviation presupposes an outside standard, an absolute in each of the four categories of tone, which the performer first masters and then treats freely. This freedom from being bound by the absolute is like a royal prerogative or being above the law. It is said to be conferred by achieving a high degree of skill or graduating into a privileged status of artistry. As we have seen, two of the objections to the deviation theory are that it fails to account for the artistry in folk music and in children, where no preliminary period of mastery of absolutes can be supposed, and that it sets no limits on the extent of deviation—indeed, associates deviation with the instability of nervous traits. The theory of the tolerance, on the contrary, needs no distinction between the folk- or child-musician and the musically trained. It shows that an absolute or the "regular" is an illusion. Actually, the "regular" in music is the result of limiting variations in performance values to the tolerance permitted by the natural salience of musical materials.

We have also referred to a third objection to the deviation theory, namely, its attempt to support the existence of absolutes by identifying them with the notes that are printed on the musical page. The notes on the page, it maintains, refer to metronomic time, true pitch, even loudness, and pure tone. In this way, the "preliminary mastery" is associated with "getting to know the printed page," and "artistry" is associated with subsequently treating the page freely and deviating from it. We have pointed out, however, that the printed page arrived on the musical scene only relatively recently. For many centuries, music was transmitted orally, and when notation was introduced it was mainly for mnemonic purposes, to recall the already known. To this day, notation retains an extensive oral supplement, and the factor of conversance with idiom still reflects the mnemonic origin.

This confusion, this attributing of absolutes to the printed page, is not confined to the deviation theory. It is much more widespread and accounts for many shortcomings in teaching methods as well as for student difficulties in reading and memorizing. To complete this exposition of the esthetics of performance, therefore, we must show the subtle relation that exists between notation and musical structure. We will then understand that the subtlety of this relationship is the reason

why the significance of the printed page has been misconstrued.

26 THE EMERGENCE OF NATURAL SALIENCE IN THE DEVELOPMENT OF NOTATION

The development of musical structure always races ahead of
notation. But when notation catches up and devises features to
match new aspects of structure, their relationship changes.
Notation then begins to suggest new structural possibilities in
much the same way that a pencil and pad help to organize
ideas and sketch plans. Therein lies the subtlety of the relationship. While the compositional process is creating needs for
notation, the act of notating, by delineating the elements of
structure graphically, is also clarifying the problems of
composition.

Let us therefore see how notation first met the basic needs of
musical structure. To fulfill the requirements of the scale,
notation borrowed the alphabet. The ancient Greeks had used
alphabetical letters to identify pitches, but the early Christian
era greatly simplified the Greek system and added two important features. It reduced the number of letters to seven, and
it drew a parallel between the succession of notes of a scale
and the succession of letters in the alphabet. As a result, moving
forward in the alphabet meant rising pitch and moving back-
ward meant descending pitch. Also, the restriction to seven
letters, A to G, gave the name of A to the eighth tone, thus
establishing the principle of naming notes an octave apart by
the same name.

This form of notation is called *alphabetical*. It sprang from an
art that in actual practice used a small pitch range and repeated
the same note many times. Ancient Greek music was of this
type, reiterating the same pitch at length before changing. The
ragas of India's music, too, were limited to a few notes, and, as
Curt Sachs says, in ancient China "emotion seems to have

emanated much more from single sounds than from melodic turns."[44] Since repeating the same note does not offer enough variety for an art form, the ancient musicians were clearly depending upon other resources for their effects. Changes in tone quality, resulting from variations in intensity and from the changing syllables that were sung, compensated for sameness of pitch. Ancient musical art, then, was vitally concerned with the natural salience of timbre.

Within the limited range that these ancient high civilizations employed, discrimination and identification of pitch was undoubtedly furthered by the mechanics of playing instruments. The position of fingers on strings or on the side-holes of pipes dramatized ascending or descending pitch. Pitch became tangible, and, since it is more stable on instruments, the singer's glide over a range of pitch was eventually changed into a traversal of definite steps. Profiting by this development, which was already well advanced, the Greeks were able to organize a system of scales that is the basis of Western music. Although their practical needs were largely met by alphabetical notation, their theoretical system of scales laid the groundwork for an art that required a second form of notation called neumatic.

Neumatic notation arose from the need to define the pitch intervals for an art that was more interested in melody than in timbre. It hit upon the ingenious device of a parallel between height in space and height in pitch. Placing one note higher on the page than another signified that it was higher in pitch, and the distance between them represented the size of the pitch interval. At first, the course of a melody was indicated by lengths of lines that slanted to the right for ascending pitch and to the left for descending. Later, the need to differentiate the number of tones in the ascent or descent of the melodic line led to dividing the slanting lines into segments, thus producing "notes." Neumatic notation, then imitates melodic line graphically and derives its names from *neumes*, a term for melodic motifs.

The development of neumatic notation is associated with the art of plainsong, or liturgical chant, in the early Christian church. The *Oxford History of Music* tells us that "the plainsong melodies were learned by ear, and singers were presumed to know them by heart; all that was required of notation was that it should remind the singer of his repertory and show him how to sing it." [45] Even when the slanted lines of neumatic notation had been segmented into notes, notation could act only as a reminder because the performer had merely indefinite spaces between the notes to represent the pitch intervals of the melodic motif or neume. Also, he could not check his pitch against instruments because the Church forbade their use in the service. It is not surprising that the Church authorities were forced, from time to time, to counteract the erosive effect of performance from remembered stimuli. In edicts and proclamations, they demanded a return to former purity of style.

The authorities were certainly helped by the addition of the horizontal line to notation. A horizontal line joining two or more notes of the melodic motif reminded the performer that they had the same pitch, and eventually, by adding more horizontal lines and forming a staff, this reminder was extended to all the notes. However, the incorporation of the staff into notation had a much greater significance than that of a check rein on the choirs. It signified the juncture of alphabetical with neumatic notation. Each line and space of the staff now had an alphabetical name, and the succession of letters in the alphabet was identified not simply with consecutive pitch but with the succession of notes in a scale. Henceforth, every melodic motif could be analyzed as an arrangement of the notes of a scale.

There is a striking similarity between the situation that the staff was designed to correct and factors in the development of folksong. Each person who sings a folksong tends to change it somewhat. Such changes can mean improvement, and they have been compared to the action of the ocean surf on a pebble, which rounds it to perfection. But they can also mean deterioration, as when the singer replaces a line he cannot remember with an incongruous one from another song. Once a folksong is written down, this process of development, whether for better or worse, immediately ceases. The fact of notating it creates a standard to which all subsequent renditions are expected to conform. The notation is not merely a reminder; it is a *forceful* reminder of how the tune goes. It signifies the end of a prior era when an improvisatory attitude held sway.

The introduction of the staff, therefore, did much more than curb alteration of the chant. Stated in our terms, it upheld the natural salience of the notes of the scale. Two notes had the same pitch because they were one note in the scale. So that the listener would regard them as having the same pitch, the performer was required to narrow their pitch difference to the point where both of them represented the one note in the scale. We see here the origin of the tolerance for pitch intervals. When notation declared the pitch in melodies to be identical with pitch intervals that already existed in nature, it gave natural salience to the pitch that was to be used in music. Undoubtedly, the effect of such an identification was restrictive, but due to the possibility of the tolerance, which permitted individual variations within an acceptable range, enough scope for individual differences was left. If the freedom to improvise was gone, the freedom to interpret remained.

There was a second and equally important reason why freedoms that existed prior to staff notation had to be given up: the advent of polyphony or the sounding of different melodies together. Polyphony requires both the performer and the composer to listen horizontally and vertically at the same time. They must hear not only the pitch intervals in one melody but also the intervals that it makes with a second melody. This requirement is so demanding that polyphony was long in coming and slow in developing. The musician must give musical sense to two or more melodic curves simultaneously, and he must also be aware of the changes in consonance or dissonance that result from the interaction of these curves. Anyone who has written music in *counterpoint*, as the oppositions of polyphony are often termed, knows what a tug-of-war ensues when the melodic curve pulls one way and the need for consonance another.

Staff notation and polyphony, then, meant a considerable loss in melodic freedom. But the compensation was a gain from the effects of consonance. If the composer was forced to forego a particular melodic line, he could draw satisfaction from altering it to sound well against other lines. The test of his ability became how well-shaped his melodies remained despite the demands for consonance that they made on each other. That is, the demands of consonance took precedence over the demands of melody and the priority of consonance was to be hidden by the skill of the composer with melody. Once this order of precedence was established, a further form of natural salience became necessary in order that the criterion of consonance could be applied. It was found in grading the pitch intervals according to their degree of consonance and relating these gradations to conditions in the simultaneous progress of the melodies. For example, the composer tended to begin and end with the most perfect consonances, the unison and the octave. And many other ways of guiding melodic flow through the channels of consonance, under the headings of *preparation* and *resolution* of degrees of dissonance, were gradually worked out. To the natural salience of the scale degrees was added the natural salience of the intervals' consonance. Two performers were in consonance because both adhered to the intervals contained in the same scale. But necessarily, the tolerance for consonance was narrower than that for solo performance.

There was a further factor, however, that the early contrapuntalists were compelled to take into account. Since the growth of polyphony was mainly under the aegis of the Church, the function of their music was still to set the texts of the church service. The conditions of the single-line plainsong had been the most favorable for melodic expression of these texts. A new situation arose when the text was shared among the plural and different lines of polyphony. The contrapuntalists discovered that when melodies based on plainsong "moved" in conformity with the demands of consonance, the moments to move were neither those of plainsong nor those that suited the accents of the words in the text. Actually, these early composers had to find a *new kind of rhythm*, a rhythm that would make the conjunction of melodies according to the demands of consonance seem appropriate to the accent of the words as well. They tried the expedient of importing existing rhythmic patterns from dance music. But this, too, was limited by how often the accent of the borrowed pattern coincided with that of the text. Besides, the text had religious associations to which a pattern of outside origin might not be suited.

What was needed was a new kind of stress. Rhythm depends upon grouping in relation to stress, and grouping means subordinating some notes to others. In plainsong, the stress that produces this subordination is basically the same as the stress in speech. Polyphony evolved a different way of subordinating. It made a virtue from the necessity for melodies to sound well together. Certain notes of one melody became subordinate to the others because they were in less consonant relation with the notes of a second melody. That is, horizontal subordination became dependent upon vertical states of consonance. The more consonant points of contact among the melodies became the stresses, and this new source of stress supplied the requisite conditions for rhythmic grouping.

The rhythm of speech, then, became secondary to the tensions in relative consonance that are created when one voice moves against another. These tensions demanded resolutions to which the arrangement of syllables in the text was required to conform. The resolutions, in turn, had the effect of establishing points of rest that offered the basis for subordinating the notes between them and thus for matching the relation of unaccented to accented syllables in speech. The composers came to think in terms of two simultaneous musical themes instead of two simultaneous notes; and when this occurred, polyphony left the infantile stage and began to grow up.

It is evident that a rhythm that arose from changing relations of consonance among melodies would place a premium on the moments when their notes changed. Any appreciable delay by one performer in moving to the next note in his melodic part would in effect produce another pitch interval, one that the composer did not desire. Some way had to be found of evaluating the duration of notes so that two or more performers would arrive at their melodic tones at the right moments to obtain the desired consonances. A long period of experimentation ensued in which the factors governing relative consonance were always uppermost. Willi Apel, in *The Notation of Polyphonic Music*, points out that "throughout the twelfth, thirteenth and fourteenth centuries, the mechanics of notation were in a state of continuous flux and rapid change, produced and paralleled by an evolution in musical style the progress of which lies mainly in the field of rhythm." [46] Also, Apel emphasizes the importance, when transcribing early scores into modern notation, of relating their note values to the principles of consonance and dissonance that existed at the time.

Again, the Church was an interested spectator during this long period of experimentation, and it was well served by the outcome. For in one sense, the experimentation involved a conflict between the rhythm resulting from relations of consonance and rhythm resulting from the regularly recurring accent of the dance. The Church, of course, was opposed to the worldly influence of the dance; and had rhythm that depends on regular accent prevailed, the spiritual achievements of polyphonic church music would not have been possible. Just as the rhythm of plainsong, deriving from the accentuation of words, could remain free from the accent of the dance, so the rhythm of polyphony, stemming from the relations of consonance among intervals, preserved the melodic curves from the upsetting effect of dance rhythms. Nevertheless, the pendulum swung back and forth between the nonperiodic ideal of the Church and the regularity of dance accent, and each borrowed from the other in order to take over advantages and adapt them to differing needs.

Finally, in the conditions surrounding the development of notation for rhythm, we must not overlook the importance of the ear's ability to estimate duration. We have said that the ear can most easily relate unequal durations when one is half or twice the other. This natural propensity was reflected in the selection of a *longa*, a long note, which was twice the duration of a *brevis* or short note, a selection that resembles the long and short syllables of versification. Once these choices were made, it was inevitable that the remaining note values would form a geometric series with them, as in the case of the soon-appearing *semibrevis*, because the entire system had to be interrelated. We may assume that the two main aspects that we have cited acted as guiding forces: the need to resolve tensions created by changing relations of consonance, and the physical movements required by varieties of the dance.

Both of these aspects, in that they involved the contents of duration, helped to measure it, and the remarkable thing is that experiences from two such diverse sources could collaborate toward the same end. In actual practice, therefore, neither the tensions of relative consonance nor the movements of the dance could always be fitted precisely into the geometric series of note values. The solution to the problem was found in the phenomenon of the tolerance, which we have already described. The ability of the ear remained the overriding consideration and gave the series of note values natural salience. Then, whenever the tensions of relative consonance or the physical movements of the dance tended either to overflow or to fail to fill the allotted durations, the slack was taken up by a permissible range of fluctuations that surrounded each note value notwithstanding the fact that its notation remained the same.

This intactness of the note value, despite the fluctuations surrounding it, is easier to observe in the case of dance music than where polyphonic rhythm is concerned. For example, the rhythmic pattern, dotted eighth note followed by sixteenth note, has appeared in music for many centuries and in conjunction with a great variety of purposes. In units of a hundred, its ratio of durations is 75 : 25. The next nearest ratios in the note value series are 66⅔ : 33⅓ for the quarter note and eighth note within a triplet on the side of longer duration and 87½ : 12½ for the double-dotted eighth note and thirty-second note on the side of shorter duration. With a tolerance of plus or minus 5 units, the performer could alter the 75 : 25 ratio of the dotted eighth and sixteenth to 80 : 20 or 70 : 30 without encroaching on tolerances for the ratios of the next nearest patterns.

When we consider how often the dotted eighth note and sixteenth note pattern has occurred and in what varieties of circumstances, we realize that it could not possibly have had the same meaning on all occasions. It has meant one thing in a minuet, another in a mazurka, another in a march, etc. With the aid of the tolerance, the performer could meet the varying requirements of these three among many compositions using the pattern without upsetting the natural salience of the note values. Indeed, the composer expects the performer to make such adjustments. He will sometimes add the indication *grazioso* to the minuet, *scherzando* to the mazurka, and *marche militaire* or even *marcia sulla morte d'un eroe* to the march. He thereby signifies that the performer is to select, within a tolerance for the 75 : 25 ratio, the ratio that is most appropriate for each of these different purposes.

The composer also signifies that such indications are in keeping with every other aspect of his composition. If every particular of his structure did not contribute to one central purpose, no amount of contextual references would achieve it for him. Had not Beethoven otherwise demonstrated that he had a funeral march in mind, by choosing minor tonality, low register, somber melodic outline, and stark phraseology, the indication "march on the death of a hero" would have been of no avail. Consequently, when performing this third movement of Beethoven's Piano Sonata No. 12 in A-flat major, Op. 26, the player takes all these structural elements into account and finds the proper ratio for the dotted-eighth and sixteenth-note pattern by relating it to their total objective. He draws upon his own experience and uses his imagination to reconstitute the measured tread of the funeral march, its somber accents, and grief-laden melody. The saliences of the score guide him toward the composer's vision, but his choice of ratios comes from his own experience, from his conviction that he has found the true echo of Beethoven's experience in his own.

This historical survey, brief as it must be, yet shows how incredibly complex the development of notation was. At each step, a further requirement of structure placed the existing symbols of notation under strain. Should new symbols be invented? For two main reasons, the answer tended to be: Adapt the old symbols to the new purposes rather than invent others. First, the existing symbols represented musical materials that already had the advantages of natural salience. For example, since the scale had already been selected from the indeterminate area of pitch, the intervals needed for polyphony were limited to the ones the scale offered. Second, however wide in scope the composer desires his expression to be, he is limited to materials with natural salience. For example, increased dissonance was drawn from the same materials that had produced the previous level. The composer is thus committed in advance to finding resemblances among his structures so that he can put the same symbol to different uses.

These two shaping forces are largely responsible for notation's extremely succinct and economical use of symbols, for the amazing power to condense that we noted in the very first chapter. It is up to the performer to detect the differences of purposes within notation of the same symbol. The tolerance may seem to offer him a small range of choices that will express the composer's varied aims with the same symbol. But in reality, it is entirely adequate as well as extremely powerful in effect. Only when notation's economy is misconstrued as a statement of absolutes will it seem to be mechanical and restrictive and suggest the mistaken idea that the performer has "licence to deviate." Natural salience gives the performer his range of choice, musical structure guides him to his selection of performance values, and the multiple significance of the same notation symbol enables him to find and express the new purposes of an innovating composer.

V THE ACHIEVEMENT OF PERFORMANCE VALUES

27 The Participation of the Listener

In this chapter we consider the remaining factor in the process of musical performance: how the listener is able to receive the composer's expression from the presentation by the performer. In the case of each of the other factors, we have dealt with negative attitudes ranging from skepticism to outright denial that musical concepts could be transmitted. We showed that there is indeed a realm of action for the performer that is in accord with physical law and that selection of performance values obeys workable principles and is not self-delusion. Here, too, we are told that direct communication with the listener does not exist, that it is an illusion created by patterns of association, by thoughts from the listener's own daily life which have been activated, not by the performance, but merely by his effort to listen. Again, since all the factors interlock, much depends on our being able to describe a recognizable and fruitful area for the listener. In order to complete the transmission from composer and performer, we must prove that the listener is by no means a bystander but actually the focal point for their entire efforts.

In giving such importance to the listener, we may at first seem to be handicapping ourselves with his possible indifference to and ignorance about the composer's and the performer's efforts.[47] Yet, the distinction here is between *the* listener and *a* listener, the same kind of distinction that is habitually made elsewhere. A building, a motor car, a tool are designed to be used by people. Some people may litter or deface the building, destroy the car and themselves in a smash-up, use a wrench to hammer. These misuses are unfortunate, but they do not change the design of the objects, which conforms to the *potential* of people in general. In the case of music, designing in terms of this potential means that music is to be understood, not simply to be heard. The composer desires the listeners not merely to hear the sounds that he presents but to make sense out of them, and therefore he constantly takes the musical dimensions of the

FIG. 38

(a)

Five,   Six,   Pick Up   Sticks

(b) Alla turca, Piano Sonata in A major, K.331, Mozart

listener into account. In short, he treats the ear as an entrance to other areas of the listener's capacity.

In Sections 16 and 25, we described some of these areas of the listener's capacity that are reached through the ear. We showed that the listener's sense of rhythm enables him to group monotonously given, evenly spaced sounds and to produce such sounds, by clapping, on his own. We can now add that he also has the power to subdivide rhythmically maintained durations into equal parts. In Fig. 38, (a) is a rhythmic pattern based on subdivision into two equal parts. People frequently clap it, and it is embodied, also, in the nursery rhyme *Five, Six, Pick Up Sticks*. It is typical of the march and may be illustrated by the last movement (*Alla turca*) of Mozart's Piano Sonata in

A major, K.331, Fig. 38(b). Subdivision into three equal parts, in the manner of *See, Saw, Margery Daw*, Fig. 39(a), is characteristic of the waltz, an example of which is given in Fig. 39(b), from Schumann's Novelette Op. 21, No. 7. It is no accident that the basic rhythmic capacities of the listener figure importantly in the formation of nursery rhymes.[48]

We should therefore expect the listener's rhythmic abilities to be the crucial factors in deciding the nature of musical continuity. The need to "take in," to absorb, will be paramount, and for this reason, music only *seems* to have continuous flow, like a stream. In reality, it is a chain made up of equal links,

Fig. 39

(a)

See   Saw   Mar-ge-ry   Daw

(b) Middle section, Novelette Op. 21, No. 7, by Schumann

and these links are the counterpart of the listener's sense of rhythm. Unless the listener treats the musical continuity as a series of linked segments, he will get very little from it. Just as he drinks water in swallows and cuts his food into bite-size pieces, so he must not allow music to stream into his ears in a continuous flow but must cause it to enter in rhythmically subdivided amounts. There is such a thing, too, as musical indigestion.

A good illustration of the links that make up the chain of music is offered by the tune of *America* (in Britain, *God Save the Queen*). Fig. 40 shows that they are two measures in length and strikingly similar rhythmically. Of the seven links, four are exactly alike in rhythm and three are closely similar. Indeed,

were it not for the changes in melody, the monotony of the
rhythm would become obvious. We are reminded here, of the
characteristic monotony of the earliest forms of music. The
primitive engaged in endless repetition of the same link. Later,
he learned to modify the links, but his practice lives on in a
basic principle of musical continuity: The links must not be
modified beyond the point of some similarity.

FIG. 40

The tune of *America* is constructed in accord with this principle. It reveals that one way of making each succeeding link
somewhat similar to the preceding is to retain the same rhythm
and change the melody. However, composers are so deeply
concerned about being understood that they are careful, as
this tune shows, to keep the links melodically similar, too. They
can again make use of the listener's innate capacities, this time
the melodic ones, such as the ability to recognize when the
successive tones of a scale rise or fall in pitch. One must be able
to detect such changes in pitch from as few as two successive

tones, and while some people at first need more, they can be easily trained to reduce the number.

The listener, then, has a basic sensitivity to changes of pitch. He can also build on this ability and group different pitches. In Fig. 41(a), the melody proceeds from one tone to the next degree above in the scale, and then the first tone reoccurs. The listener will remember the first tone and register the fact that the third tone has the same pitch. He will say that the melody *returned* to the same pitch, and this perception of a return groups the three tones together. The result would be much the same if the middle tone were the second degree above in the scale, Fig. 41(b). The only difference would be that the listener

FIG. 41

would consider the first and second tones further related by their harmoniousness.

Fig. 42(a) and (b) illustrate the listener's melodic and rhythmic comprehension during the course of the familiar tune *Silent Night*. His sense of rhythm and the identity of measures 1 and 2 tell him that the links are one measure in size. The rhythmic similarity of the links is shown at (b). Examining the melody in (a) for groups, we see the two designs presented in Fig. 41: In measure 1, the first three notes constitute a return-ing-note group and the fourth note creates the skip to the harmonic tone below. Measure 2 repeats measure 1. Measure 3 changes the level of pitch and deletes the sixteenth note but is otherwise similar to measure 1. Measure 4 is similar to measure 3 except for the increased size of the skip. Measure 5 is more complicated, but the listener soon realizes that the direction of the skip has been reversed and the dotted rhythm has shifted to the second half of the measure. Measures 6, 7, and 8 repeat previously heard measures. Measure 9 is similar to measure 5 except that the skip is now included in the dotted-eighth pattern. Measure 10 is simply the upward skip to the harmonic tone above. Measure 11 is a conventional ending that nevertheless adheres to the rhythmic pattern and the descending skips.

In order to insure the listener's comprehension, then, music presents a continuity of links that he is to *compare* for similarities and differences. These acts of comparison can be conscious, but since the listener is to place the detection of

FIG. 42
Silent Night

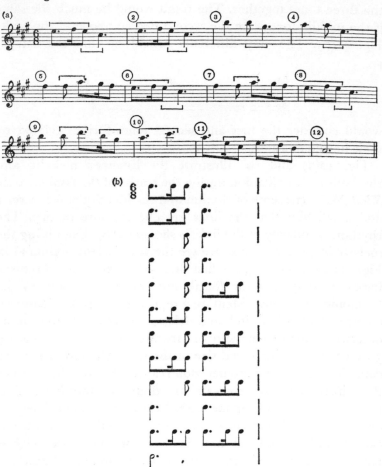

similarity and difference at the disposal of other musical purposes, they must eventually become unconscious. That is, the composer has further purposes with his links beyond supplying food for comparison, and to achieve them he depends squarely upon the detection of similarity and difference from link to link. We shall call the amount of difference and similarity between adjacent links the *rate of change* in design.

28 THE FOREGROUND AS COMPLEXITY

In Fig. 43(a) are the first two measures of Mozart's Piano Sonata in A major, K.331. At (b), the foreground of the melody

FIG. 43

(a) Measures 1 and 2, Piano Sonata in A major, K.331, by Mozart

has been reduced by analysis, revealing a substratum or background and three superimposed layers. Placing one staff above another in this fashion signifies that the theme as Mozart presented it was already a complex of layers. As such it represented Mozart's judgment of the listener's ability. Fig. 43(c) shows what Mozart would have had to do if he had felt that the listener would not immediately comprehend his theme. In telescoping the eight measures of (c) into the two measures of (a), the composer displayed confidence in the listener's ability to penetrate the three superimposed layers to the background, without the elucidation offered by (c). That his confidence was justified is attested by our description of the listener's rhythmic and melodic processes in the case of *Silent Night*, a tune that resembles the theme of the Mozart Sonata. In (a), the similarity of the two measures enables the rhythmic sense of the listener again to decide that the links are one measure in size. And again, too, he will perceive the returning-note group as well as the skip to the harmonic note above.

Such layered construction without further explanation, which is typical of all music, suggests that we refer to the foreground in terms of its *complexity*. This method of qualifying the foreground is useful because any one of the four staves in (b) could have been the foreground of a composition. We can refer to the foreground's *degree* of complexity and say that one theme is more complex than another because it resulted from more superimposed layers. Fig. 43(d) illustrates this approach in terms of increasing complexity, since the movement of the Sonata is a theme and variations, by placing the first measure of several variations in comparison with the theme. Clearly, the foreground of each variation is more complex than that of the theme.

It should not be supposed, however, that a more complex foreground is for that reason a better one. The variations in (d) are not better or more desirable music than the theme. In analogy to the biological theory of evolution, which recognizes that one organism can be more complex than another without being considered superior to it, we shall call this characteristic of the foreground *evolutionary* complexity.[49] Evolutionary complexity refers to the finality and intactness of different foregrounds whatever their degree of complexity or the number of layers in their construction. The degree of complexity will be proportional to the number of superimposed layers and will represent a judgment of the listener's capacity to penetrate them and reach the background. But it is evolutionary in the sense that it does not confer superiority on one theme over another.

The meaning of evolutionary complexity, the significance of refraining from evaluations on the basis of superiority, becomes even clearer when we move beyond comparison of variations within the same composition to comparison of themes by different composers which, curiously, are sometimes built on the same background. In Fig. 44, staff II is the theme of the last movement of Beethoven's Piano Sonata No. 25 in G major, Op. 79; staff III, the opening bars of his Piano Sonata No. 30 in E major, Op. 109; and staff IV, the theme of Chopin's Etude in G-flat major, Op. 25, No. 9. For purposes of comparison, these

FIG. 44

three themes have been placed in G major and related to staff I, which shows that they have the same or a closely similar background. Despite their common background, each is an intact organism. One may be more complex than the other, but it is not therefore superior.

The listener's penetration of evolutionary complexity bears a strong resemblance to the process of *cancellation* in reducing fractions to lower terms. For example, given the fraction 1218/2436, one might first reduce it with the factor 2: 609/1218. Then, applying the factor 3, the result is 203/406. At this point, the absence of factors would lead to a direct comparison of the two numbers and reveal the lowest term to be 1/2. Similarly, in Fig. 43(b), staff II shows that reducing a passage melodically means to cancel out subsidiary tones, such as passing tones, neighboring tones, and appoggiaturas. Reducing a passage rhythmically, as in staff III, is accomplished by eliminating all notes but those on main beats. Staff IV illustrates harmonic reduction, which consists in divesting the passage of notes that duplicate the component tones of chords. Just as an infinite number of fractions are possible as higher terms of 1/2, so an infinite number of foregrounds may be constructed on a given background. Also, just as this infinite number of possible fractions have the same value of 1/2, so all the possible foregrounds on the given background have exactly the same "value" or status as long as the sole basis for judging their status is their degree of complexity.

Considering Mozart's theme from another point of view, Fig. 43(b) shows that there are four layers in the complexity of measure 2 as well as in that of measure 1. That is, the four acts of comparison that are implied in penetrating the foreground of staff I to reach the background of staff IV are also implied in reducing measure 2. But in the case of measure 2, a new type of comparison comes into play. The fact that it is preceded by measure 1 is vitally important to the continuity. Having created evolutionary complexity for both measures, the composer must also have related them in some way. He may have created two links, but they must both belong to the same chain. This is the point where what we have termed the *rate of change* operates. The composer relates the two measures by proportioning their differences to their similarities. A judicious rate of change carries the listener from link to link, permitting him to perceive the similarities and differences, such as those that we explained in the analysis of *Silent Night*. The disruption that too great a rate of change would cause in the listener is illustrated in Fig. 43(e), where the second measure of variation VI has been placed next to the first measure of the theme. Both this borrowed measure and the opening one are products of evolutionary complexity. Their foregrounds are equally final and intact results of superimposed layers. But their differences far outweigh their similarities and the continuity is upset.

There is therefore a second type of complexity that has to do with the relation from link to link as opposed to evolutionary complexity, which is concerned with the intrinsic structure of each link. We shall call this second type *organic complexity*. It views measures in the chain of continuity as *adjacent*, as *prior* and *subsequent*, in contrast to their structure as individual entities. It estimates the rate of change, or ratio of difference to similarity, between prior and subsequent links.

Accordingly, organic complexity is concerned with the influence of the prior link on the construction of the subsequent. This influence is naturally greatest when the subsequent link repeats the prior exactly. But exact repetition can easily become boring, and two other ways have been devised of gaining its advantages without risking loss of interest. One of these is use of the sequence, which the two measures of Mozart's theme illustrate. To create a sequence, the evolutionary complexity of the subsequent link must be identical with that of the prior, and the organic difference between them must be confined to a parallel shift of all the constituent tones to other degrees of the scale. The second way is to use some features of the sequence but allow harmonic considerations to take precedence over melodic. Fig. 45, the opening bars of Bach's Prelude No. 1 in C major from Book I of the *Well-tempered Clavier*, explains this method. Here, the melodic intervals of the succession of notes are altered to conform to harmonies that are not in themselves sequential. The evolutionary complexities of the prior and subsequent measures are identical, but their organic complexity, or rate of change from link to link, is entirely governed by the harmonic progression underlying the composition.

The listener, therefore, engages in two types of comparison to solve the two types of complexity. In the case of evolutionary complexity, his acts of comparison may be called "vertical" because they progress from the complexity of the foreground to the simplicity of the background. The vertical factor in comparison or penetration is most clearly illustrated by the very first link of a composition, for there the background is reached without help from the subsequent links.

Since vertical penetration is dependent on the listener's ability, we must realize that we have here a more advanced

Fig. 45

Prelude No. 1 in C major, Well-tempered Clavier, Book I, by Bach

form of what once was simpler. This circumstance is illustrated by Fig. 43(c), which we said Mozart would have been forced to write had he distrusted the comprehension of the listener. It presents the steps, as an organic continuity with a minimum rate of change, that are required for penetration of the evolutionary complexity. We may therefore conclude that the process that produces evolutionary complexity *telescopes* relationships that at one time were organic and then represented the limit of the listener's powers of perception. Later, when through use and familiarity these relationships became easier for him to perceive, there was no longer any necessity to present them organically, or one after the other, and they were combined into the simultaneous presentation that is characteristic of evolutionary complexity.

For the solution of organic complexity, the listener's acts of comparison are of a second type termed *horizontal* instead of vertical. His activity may be called horizontal because he relates subsequent to prior links as, so to speak, they pass in review before him and he detects the amount of change from one to the next by their similarities and differences. This rate of change from link to link, and hence the degree of organic complexity, increases progressively from the one extreme of exact repetition to the opposite extreme of highly contrapuntal music. Half way between these extremes are the sequences and the harmonically dominated links that we cited in Mozart's Sonata K.331 and Bach's First Prelude respectively. In general, Bach's preludes are less complex organically than his fugues, although he demands more and more of the listener's horizontal acts of comparison with each succeeding prelude. Still, Bach was aware of the effort that is required to penetrate and relate adjacent links and he was careful to keep to the same format of evolutionary complexity for long periods of time and often throughout the composition.

29   FOREGROUND REDUNDANCY

Sequences and harmonically dominated links depend upon a high degree of repetition and, when they are used, the rate of change from link to link will naturally be small. The links will be closely similar, and the listener will need only a minimum of effort to detect the differences from one link to the next. It follows, too, if the close similarity is extended over a number of links, that the listener will need less and less effort to detect the differences. This circumstance is illustrated by Fig. 43(f), which continues the organic relation of sequence in Mozart's two measures for three more. After the third measure or link, the listener will withdraw his conscious attention from the continuity and, as we have already noted in another connection, will treat it as a continuing stimulus. He expects the sequence to continue indefinitely and will not reapply his conscious attention until the continuity changes. In short, he has become accustomed to a *fixed* rate of change from prior to subsequent links.

There is an unwritten law in composition, therefore, that a faithful sequence should not continue for more than three links. Beyond that point, the listener withdraws conscious attention, and the musical continuity would be considered not sufficiently stimulating. It has become, as we shall term it, *redundant*. The term *redundant* is especially appropriate here because it can be applied in two senses—one, praiseworthy, and the other, fault-finding. In its praiseworthy sense, it means "luxuriant" or "copious"; in its fault-finding sense, it means "excessive" or "superfluous." The example in Fig. 43(f) is certainly redundant in the sense of "excessive." Yet, the tendency of the listener to relegate the redundant to a lower level of consciousness, to treat sequences and harmonically dominated links as continuing stimuli, is a very powerful aid to the composer and, after him, to the performer. It grants them the opportunity of applying further stimuli to the listener without cutting off the original stimulus, which has become redundant, or in this sense "luxuriant" instead of "excessive."

From this point of view, the listener should be visualized as a multilevel organism that is capable of carrying on several activities simultaneously. Such an image of the individual is by no means strange. We can easily recall instances of multileveled activity—for example, two people engaging in earnest conversation while walking in the rain, holding an umbrella overhead, avoiding puddles, not losing their way, etc. Let us then see how the listener absorbs other stimuli without losing track of the continuing ones. In Bach's First Prelude, Fig. 45, the second half of each measure repeats the first half. In addition, the organic complexity from measure to measure is the harmonically dominated type that we have described as a modified form of sequence. Consequently, by the fourth measure, two elements of the foreground will have become redundant: (1) the rhythmic pattern of eight sixteenth notes per half measure, and (2) the melodic outline made by these sixteenths. The listener will conclude that the two elements can be expected to continue, and he will look for some *further* organic relation between the links.

Since the listener is comparing links, his attention will be drawn to the moments when the differences from link to link occur. Bach has been careful to make these moments of change coincide with the voice-leading of a five-part harmonic progression, Fig. 46. In this figure, the parts have been numbered from the lowest upward: Part I will always be the first of the eight sixteenth notes in the half measure, part II will always

FIG. 46

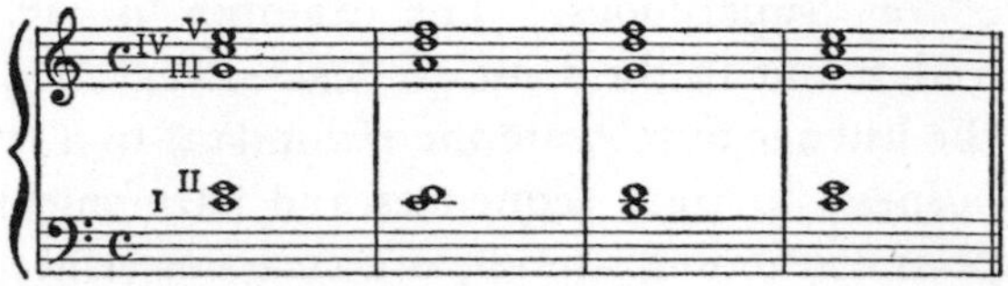

be the second, part III the third, etc. By relating the first note in measure 1 to the first note in measure 2, the second note in measure 1 to the second in measure 2, etc., the listener becomes aware of both the harmonic progression and the voice-leading in Fig. 46. The detection of Fig. 46 becomes the further stimulus while the rhythm and the melodic outline of the eight notes of each half measure remain continuing stimuli at a lower level of consciousness. The organic redundancy of these eight notes has permitted the listener's acts of comparison to deal with a more remote or higher order of relationship between the prior and subsequent links. These circumstances define precisely what is meant by a pattern of asynchronization.

It is evident that the possibilities of organic redundancy offer the composer a wide variety of characters or moods simply by changing the pattern of asynchronization. As Fig. 47(a) (b) (c) shows, he can obtain the effects of a polonaise, a waltz, and a mazurka, respectively, by adapting the asynchronization to the traditional rhythms of these dances. Such rhythms are more distinctive than the continual sixteenth notes of Bach's Prelude, but they, too, become redundant. Their fixed rate of change from measure to measure causes the listener to submerge them to a less conscious level and again to derive the five-part progression at his most aware level. There is no difference from

FIG. 47

his attitude toward the Prelude beyond his acceptance of the added connotations of polonaise, waltz, and mazurka.

During the second half of the 18th century, composers took advantage of the multilevel predisposition of the listener to contrive a special form of melody-accompaniment relationship. In this form, the patterns of asynchronization are highly stylized. They easily become a continuing stimulus, and a more freely moving melody may be superimposed upon the implied parts of the progression. The listener is then stimulated by two simultaneous rates of change, that of the asynchronization, which is *fixed*, and that of the melody, which *fluctuates*. He engages in two simultaneous acts of comparison, one that convinces him that the pattern of asynchronization will not change and another that reveals to him the differences and similarities from link to link of the melody. This special type of arrangement, again in the context of polonaise, waltz, and mazurka, is illustrated in Fig. 48(a) (b) (c).

The awareness of the theme in the treble remained conscious

FIG. 48

due to the fluctuating rate of change, whereas the awareness of the asynchronization in the bass became subconscious because the rate of change was fixed. It was precisely this difference between a conscious and an unconscious awareness that prompted the designations melody versus accompaniment. Although the development of the melody-accompaniment relation is associated with the latter half of the 18th century, it may be said to be anticipated by the need in counterpoint to subordinate one voice to another. Sometimes, too, the subordinate contrapuntal voice has a harmonic cast, as in the case of the bass in Bach's Prelude No. 10 in E minor from Book I of the *Well-tempered Clavier*, Fig. 49, and it seems to have purely the function of an accompaniment. However, on closer examination, we see that Bach has not asynchronized the sixteenth notes of the bass but has written them in two-part counterpoint with the treble voice.

As we observe the different kinds of relationship that the concept of evolutionary complexity makes possible, we are impressed anew by the finality of a foreground whatever its degree of complexity. Thus, the foreground of a folksong, sung

FIG. 49
Prelude No. 10 in E minor, Well-tempered Clavier, Book I, by Bach

by one singer without accompaniment, is as final or complete as the foreground of a symphony, played by a full complement of orchestral musicians. In view of this circumstance, this intactness of a foreground whatever its complexity, we may well wonder whether there is any limit to how complex a foreground may be or even why composers progressively increased the complexity of the foreground from that of the folksong to that of the symphony. There must have been at least two factors that acted as brakes upon the tendency toward increasing complexity: (1) the ability of the listener to penetrate the number of layers that were superimposed upon the background, and (2) an interference between one layer and another when a larger number of them were involved. Yet foreground complexity did increase steadily, showing that these two factors were peripheral and that the explanation of what governs the degree of foreground complexity lies elsewhere.

We can find the explanation of increasing foreground complexity with the aid of a simple device: Since we are contrasting the proportions of a folksong with full, symphonic-type presentation, let us select a familiar melody that is sung as often

FIG. 50
The Star-spangled Banner

unaccompanied as in fully harmonized form and compare the objectives and effect in each case. We shall then be able to determine what is gained by increasing the complexity of the foreground. A tune that satisfies these requirements is *The Star-spangled Banner*, Fig. 50(a). Since its opening phrase consists of intervals that are drawn from the tonic chord, it offers complete harmony as well as complete rhythm and melody. That is, it compresses the three components of music—harmony, rhythm, and melody—into one element, a single line, and, therefore, when it is sung unaccompanied it still gives the impression of a complete presentation.

Fig. 50(b) shows the form a foreground would take if this compression into a single line were to be avoided. A new soprano part would convey the melodic implications; an alto would present the rhythm; and the harmony would be derived from the progression of the tenor and bass parts. Three components would be needed in the foreground to match the three elements of music. The result is not as condensed as the single line of (a) but the presentation may still be termed economical.

Consider, then, the foreground in Fig. 50(c), which is the form in which the song appears in most songbooks for communal singing. This type of presentation is anything but economical. All the lines or parts join in enunciating the rhythm. The middle parts duplicate the harmonic impression that the melody itself is capable of giving. They also follow and supplement the melody's contour. It is as if each member of a group of singers insisted upon contributing to all three elements of music rather than accepted responsibility for the rhythm or harmony or the melody. We may therefore call the familiar foreground in (c) *overdetermined*. The contribution of the components in the presentation is twice-over or thrice-over to rhythm or melody or harmony. They are rhythmically or melodically or harmonically redundant. Since this second type of redundancy is clearly dependent upon an attitude during the construction of evolutionary complexity, we shall term it *evolutionary redundancy*.

Evolutionary redundancy is produced, then, whenever the composer does not differentiate the components of the foreground according to their contribution to rhythm, melody, and harmony. And we can readily understand why he so often does not differentiate them in this manner. Since he frequently has a theme before starting to compose, it may already and by itself make sizable contributions to all three elements, rhythm, melody, and harmony. As a result, anything further that he adds to the foreground when he is setting the theme will over-contribute to the three elements. To illustrate this over-determination of the foreground further, the bass in Fig. 51, from Chopin's Prelude in B minor, Op. 28, No. 6, already contains all that the listener needs to derive the three elements. Consequently, the notes in the treble staff are redundant harmonically and rhythmically. Similarly, the treble of Bach's

FIG. 51
Prelude in B minor, Op. 28, No. 6, by Chopin

FIG. 52
Prelude No. 11 in F major, Well-tempered Clavier, Book I, by Bach

Prelude, No. 11 in F major, Fig. 52, from Book I of the *Well-tempered Clavier*, completely fulfills the rhythmic, melodic, and harmonic requirements of music and thus the bass is har-monically and rhythmically redundant.

What does the composer gain from evolutionary redundancy or overdetermination of the foreground? The answer to this question, as in the case of organic redundancy, is contained in the effects upon and the natural predispositions of the listener.

As he goes through the experience of penetrating the foreground, he will receive the effect of whatever each layer adds to the presentation as it is superimposed upon the background. He will then focus conscious attention upon the nonredundant elements of the foreground and relegate the redundant elements to a subconscious level of awareness. Since the activity of penetration creates a hierarchy of complexity, the more complex layers will reiterate, in obedience to the composers' intention, what is already contained in the simpler layers. Consequently, if a more complex layer consists of both rhythmic and harmonic components and a simpler layer already fulfills the harmonic requirement, the listener will regard their combined harmonic contribution as redundant and focus his conscious attention on the rhythmic contribution. Or he will become consciously aware of some further, more remote outcome of the foreground's design, such as the movement of parts outlining an implied harmonic progression, which the redundancy renders evident. A good illustration of this subordination of immediate to more remote perceptions was Chopin's Etude in E major, Op. 10, No. 3, in Figs. 12 and 13. We can now point out that the lulling effect of rocking motion that Chopin obtained was produced by the redundancy of the foreground.

30 VARIOUS EXAMPLES OF FOREGROUND
    REDUNDANCY

At this point, it will be helpful to have further illustrations of the composer's aims with redundancy. Without becoming overly technical, we can explain how the performer reasons with the aid of perceptions of redundancy and reaches decisions about the composer's intention. The principle he follows is to treat repetitiousness in the rhythmic, melodic, and harmonic elements that make up a given link as the sign of further expressive purpose. If the music not only starts with a full chord but uses the same chordal tones for the ensuing melodic theme, he can be sure that at the moment harmony is not carrying the main burden of expression. Constant repetition of a rhythmic motif is often a sign that the harmonies underlying a passage are being asynchronized and therefore that an overlying melodic line should be located and given importance. When he must decide between two voices that seem equally important, priority is given to the one that the composer has continued beyond the other. Also, when the evaluation of redundancy suggests two possible modes of accent, the one that would be incongruous with other decisions about the passage is rejected.

(1) The third movement of Beethoven's Piano Sonata No. 4 in E-flat major, Op. 7. Fig. 53(a) shows that the initial link comprises four measures. At the very outset, Beethoven strikes a full chord. Should the notes immediately following belong to the same harmony—and in this instance they do—they will be harmonically redundant. Also, the quarter notes of measure 1 establish 3/4 time sufficiently to make measure 2 rhythmically redundant. The listener, therefore, will look beyond these overdeterminations of harmony and rhythm for a further relationship. He finds it in the contrary motion of the soprano and bass melodic lines. Beethoven, with the aid of harmonic and rhythmic redundancy, has made melodic contrary motion the *salient characteristic* of his theme. The listener responds by placing harmonic and rhythmic stimuli at a lower level of awareness than his attention level for melodic stimuli. And in terms of the

FIG. 53
Allegro, Piano Sonata No. 4 in E-flat major, Op. 7, by Beethoven

Minore section, from the same movement

context or character of the theme, his main impression will be one of graceful, arching contour.

The remaining question about which of the contrary melodic lines has the greater salience is decided by measure 3. Since at that point the melodic motion of the bass ceases and that of the soprano continues and introduces a motif in eighth notes besides, the soprano must have greater salience than the bass.

(2) The *Minore* section from the same movement. The initial link, Fig. 53(b), again contains four measures. Its construction belongs to the same type as that of Bach's Prelude in C major (Fig. 45). The rhythm and upward melodic motion of the first triplet become redundant and the triplet turns into a pattern of asynchronization. The listener soon perceives the composer's further, more remote objective, namely, the melodic motion in six parts, Fig. 53(c), three of which are duplicates at the octave. In this instance, too, the question whether part I or

part IV of the six parts in (c) has the greater salience is decided in favor of part IV because its melodic motion continues importantly beyond the eleventh measure of the section whereas that of part I ceases at that point. The similar question requiring a decision between part IV and part VI is made against part VI because, as Fig. 53(b) shows, it would accentuate the third note of each triplet. Each accentuation would create a syncopated effect which, unlike the excerpt from Mendelssohn in Fig. 36, would be out of place in this *Minore* section and conflict with the somber effect of the melodic lines in (c). Besides, Beethoven himself has precluded syncopation by placing the double *sforzando* at the very beginning of measure 3.

(3) Ballade in D minor, Op. 10, No. 1, by Brahms, Fig. 54(a) (b). All six parts state the same rhythm. Melodically, parts II, IV, and VI present the same theme in different registers, as the second example in (b) shows. The third example in (b) brings out that part V follows this melodic contour at a distance of a third and that parts I and III have the harmonic function of providing the bass, in octaves, for the tonic and dominant chords. There is redundancy, therefore, in all three categories of rhythm, melody, and harmony. Such extensive redundancy points to the purpose of creating synthetic timbre. The procedure is analogous to orchestration of the reduced form which appears in the first example of (b).

FIG. 54
Ballade in D minor, Op. 10, No. 1, by Brahms

(a)

(b)

(c) Scherzo, Piano Concerto No. 2 in B-flat major, Op. 83, by Brahms

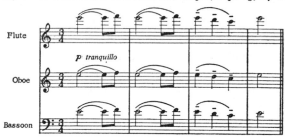

(d) La Cathédrale engloutie, by Debussy

The questions of relative salience are decided as follows: in favor of parts II—IV—VI over part V, the alto, because it ceases at the first quarter of measure 2, before the phrase ends; against parts I—III because their harmonic function confines them to two notes. Accordingly, parts II—IV—VI are given the greatest salience, and, in order to further the objective of synthetic timbre, they are treated as constituting one timbre. The point of view is the same as that governing the orchestral effect of Fig. 54(c), which occurs in the scherzo movement of Brahms's Piano Concerto No. 2 in B-flat major, Op. 83.

A similar but even more striking instance of synthetic timbre appears in the well-known passage in *La Cathédrale engloutie*, Fig. 54(d), the tenth of Debussy's Preludes, Book I. In analogy to orchestral doubling, the grouping of the parts is as follows: parts II—V—VIII, parts III—VI—IX, and parts IV—VII, as shown following the third measure. The decision about greatest salience is made between the first two groups of parts because they are doubled twice whereas parts IV—VII are doubled only once. It is made in favor of III—VI—IX because in the echo effect at the close of the piece their melodic line receives the doubling in octaves, giving it precedence over the other parts.

(4) The Prelude of Bach's English Suite No. 3 in G minor, Fig. 55. We shall use this example as typical of much of Bach's music whether he intended it for the harpsichord and organ or for instruments like the clavichord, strings, and human voice that permit greater detail of tonal variety. In the case of the organ and harpsichord, a decision is often necessary whether to play each hand on a different manual or keyboard and thereby obtain contrasting tone colors, and this kind of analysis will be found helpful in making such decisions. The large, numbered brackets, 1, 2, and 3, indicate that the links are two measures in size, starting from the second eighth note of one measure and extending into the third measure beyond. Also, they are identical except that they occupy progressively lower

registers or pitch ranges. This identity makes them redundant rhythmically and melodically and enables Bach to direct attention to the changes in register.

Why he is interested in the descending pitch of the bass becomes clear from his treatment of the treble. There bracket D introduces sixteenth notes which are rhythmically salient due to the redundancy of the eighths in bracket 2. Yet the sequential arrangement of the sixteenths in brackets E, F, and G confers rhythmic and melodic redundancy on them. Their steadily rising pitch registers become evident and contrast

FIG. 55
Prelude, English Suite No. 3 in G minor, by Bach

effectively with the descent of the bass. Bach shows us that the total effect of the passage is to be cumulative toward a goal in the sixth measure and he has underlined his purpose by adding harmonic notes to the bass. Meanwhile, he has limited the passage's harmony to two chords, the tonic and the dominant, and by alternating them uses harmonic redundancy to bring out the opposing motion still further.

(5) Schubert's Moment Musical in F minor, Op. 94, No. 5. Fig. 56(a) contains measures 1 through 4, and (b) measures 13

through 17. The four-measure link in (a) is characterized by a high degree of rhythmic and harmonic redundancy: the same rhythmic pattern in each measure and restriction of the harmony to two chords, the tonic and the subdominant. The initial, strong impression of rhythm and harmony is therefore quickly referred to a lower level of consciousness, and the melodic line of the soprano becomes salient. In general, the effect is one of synthetic timbre, but the allotment of five parts to the quarter notes and four parts to the eighths differentiates

FIG. 56

(a) Measures 1–4, Moment Musical in F minor, Op. 94, No. 5, by Schubert

(b) Measures 13–17

the downbeats from the upbeats. It is this differentiation that prevents the five-part quarter-note chords in measures 15 through 17 of (b) from being rhythmically redundant. On both upbeat and downbeat they have the power that in (a) was possessed only by downbeats, and Schubert has heightened the impression of their power by reducing or thinning measures 13 and 14 to three parts.

(6) Brahms's Rhapsody in E-flat major, Op. 119, No. 4, Fig. 57, shows certain resemblances to the Moment Musical in

Fig. 56. Measures 1–4 are analogous to Schubert's measures
1–4, and measure 5 is analogous to measures 15–17 of the
Moment Musical. The chief difference lies in Brahms's harmonization, which allots separate chords to the soprano line
throughout the five measures. This type of harmonization
gives a more ponderous effect and acts to strengthen the second
beat of each measure in contrast to the weakened second beats
of Schubert's treatment. Nevertheless, as the bass part clearly
shows, Brahms has been careful to return on the last chord of
each measure to the harmony of the first chord, a device that
weakens the force of the second beat. Therefore, he, too, gains
a nonredundant rhythmic effect from measure 5, where the

Fig. 57
Rhapsody in E-flat major, Op. 119, No. 4, by Brahms

upbeats appear appreciably strengthened, an effect that is
enhanced by his utilization of five-measure phrases. To sum
up the comparison of the two works, Brahms's harmonization
creates less harmonic redundancy than Schubert's, but, due
to the return to the same harmony at the end of each measure
that it began with, there is sufficient redundancy to give the
soprano line again greatest salience.

(7) Harmonizing each note of a melody in this way recalls
Debussy's procedures as illustrated by Fig. 58, the opening
measures of *Canope*, the Prelude No. 10 in Book II. Here, the
harmonic redundancy is that of synthetic timbre resulting from
the identical position of each chord or the parallel motion of
the four parts. Yet the effect is somewhat different from the one

cited in the composer's *La Cathédrale engloutie* because the relationships among the chords are more remote. The harmony,
therefore, retains a certain salience within his main objective,
an arching melodic line, an objective that he confirms with the

FIG. 58
Canope, by Debussy

unharmonized statement in measures 5 and 6. The redundancy
of the constant quarter notes only increases the salience of the
melodic factor.

31   THE EVALUATION OF FOREGROUND REDUNDANCY

The discussion of foreground redundancy has shown that the
salient characteristics of passages emerge from two conditions,
the similarities from link to link, and the overdetermination of
the foreground. The similarities from link to link, which we have
called organic redundancy, are disclosed to the listener by his
acts of horizontal comparison. They then become continuing
stimuli, which render differences from link to link evident and
cause the listener to seek more remote relationships among
them. The overdetermination of the foreground, on the contrary, is discovered by vertical acts of comparison, by comparing
one layer with another as the listener penetrates the super-

imposed layers to the background. As he traverses and compares these layers, he finds that their harmonic or rhythmic or melodic components are variously overproduced. This overproduction, which we have termed evolutionary redundancy, acts to reduce the individuality of the contribution a layer may make to the foreground structure and induces the listener to seek among the layers for more remote relationships that will reveal the composer's design.

The composer, on his part, is extremely careful in his calculations of both types of foreground redundancy. In the case of evolutionary redundancy, he knows that if he superimposes too many layers in the construction of any one link, the listener will bog down in the effort to penetrate them and will fail to recognize the organic relations between prior and subsequent links. In the case of organic redundancy, he knows that too high a rate of change from link to link, even when he has made penetration relatively easy, will overtax the listener's ability to derive salient characteristics from the passage.

It follows from this need for solicitude about the listener's activity of penetration that the manner in which the performer renders the passage will also either facilitate or hamper the acts of comparison. If the performer emphasizes the rhythm of a foreground that is already redundant rhythmically, he will block the listener from deriving the melody or harmony properly. When the salient characteristic of a passage is melodic contrary motion, as in Fig. 53(a), and the performer overemphasizes the treble at the expense of the bass, the listener will miss the point of the structure. In cases such as those of Fig. 45 and Fig. 53(b), where the foreground consists of patterns of asynchronization, treating each pattern as a rhythm or a melody in itself will prevent the listener from deriving the remote relationships that result from implied harmonic progression or voice-leading.

Clearly, then, the performer must be as highly skilled in the psychology of musical listening as the composer is. He must be extremely sensitive to the rate of change from link to link, to the moment when a stimulus becomes continuing, and to the signs of overdetermination of the foreground and their significance. In short, he must create the actual, physical conditions of salience for the score's potential conditions of salience. To this end, he will be helped by the built-in redundancy of the score and by the listener's capacity for multilevel awareness. Yet the appropriateness of his rendition will depend upon how successfully he relates the two, upon how well he relates the score's potential for salience to the levels of awareness in the listener.

The performer, therefore, occupies a midway point that calls for great delicacy of judgment and adjustment. The physical levels of salience that he achieves represent his interpretation of the score's potential for salience in terms of the listener's levels of awareness. For example, when performing the *Minore* section, Fig. 53(b) and (c), he first creates a level of greater salience for those tones of the treble staff that are marked with dashes (in parentheses because they were not so marked by Beethoven) and a level of lesser salience for all the remaining tones. These are the levels of prosaic salience for which, we have said, he must rely ultimately on conversance with idiom. At the first tone, A-flat, of measure 3, however, where Beethoven has placed the *sforzando*, the level of emphasis is suddenly increased for the purpose of poetic salience. This sudden increase betokens an emotional accent the extent of which rests with the judgment and sensitivity of the performer. Apparently, Beethoven desired a sizable accent because he has used a double *sforzando*, but the performer must take into account a context that is both somber and *pianissimo*.

The performer then considers the local, physical determinants of salience. First, there is the register of the initial G-flat in the treble, which is naturally strong. But the register of the E-flat in the bass, which occurs at the same moment, is also strong, and care must be exercised to subdue this tone. Next, there is the fact that the G-flat will be reiterated on the three following beats and will be reinforced as well by the G-flats that lie an octave above. In the meantime, the B-flats in both staves are reinforcing each other, and since they do not change with the changes of chords, they are apt to become overprominent. Yet the problem of keeping the triplet pattern from becoming a melody in itself is considerably eased by the preceding decisions, which have resulted in the salience of the first G-flat.

To arrive at durations for the tones of this passage, the performer keeps in mind the melodic format of Fig. 53(c). That is, the beat of this format, which is one per measure, will take precedence over the quarter-note beats of the triplets since they are patterns of asynchronization. Assuming a tempo of quarter note equals 180, or 180 quarters per minute, let us say for numerical convenience that one-beat-per-measure duration will equal 99/100ths of a second (a dotted half note would equal 60 on the metronome). This device enables us to refer to the duration of quarter notes as 33/100ths of a second and to that of the eighth notes within triplets as 11/100ths of a second.

The tolerance for the duration of the first triplet must be very small because it is essential to establish the rhythm of the formula or pattern of asynchronization. Once this rhythm is established, the tolerances for the three following triplets can be larger because they will become a continuing stimulus, and it is only necessary to remind the listener of their presence. However, F, at the asterisk on the second quarter of measure 2, must be located precisely because it marks the resumption of the main melody and, in a rhythmic way, prepares the way for the *sforzando* of measure 3. The tolerance for the duration of this F is therefore small.

To illustrate these requirements, the diagram in Fig. 59 offers a possible distribution of durations for all four measures of Fig. 53(b). The initial upbeat can have a longer duration than the 33/100ths of a second, the value that we said a quarter note would receive. The longer duration is possible because the tempo does not truly begin until the downbeat of measure 1, and it creates an effect of introduction or of preparation for the new section that is to come. The various distributions of duration for the triplets following the downbeat signify that their rhythm, given that of the first triplet, will be taken for granted. Thus, the durations of their eighth notes become available for other purposes, such as reinforcement and tone color. There is considerable leeway because the distributions for the nearest note values are sufficiently distant. For example, the distribution for two sixteenth notes and an eighth, into which a faulty performance of triplets might lapse, is roughly 8—8—16. Consequently, the various distributions of 33/100ths of a second in Fig. 59 are not in danger of being confused with it.

As the brackets for each triplet show, we have kept to a total

Fig. 59

of 33/100ths of a second for each of them. This adherence to the same total is not entirely necessary. The totals within each measure could vary, along the lines of 33—35—34 or 30—36—33. What is necessary is that the combined total of the first four triplets be very close to 132/100ths of a second. Also, the total duration of measures 1 and 2 should be close to 198/100ths of a second. The total of 132/100ths of a second offers the equivalent of 4 × 33/100 and the total of 198/100ths of a second matches 6 × 33/100. Thus, on one side, the limit for the tolerances governing the distribution of durations is avoidance of confusion with other note values and, on the other, the maintenance of total durations that are in keeping with the main beats and with the main design of the structure.

It is important that the distribution of durations in Fig. 59 is not confused with *tempo rubato*, which is a device of doubtful validity. *Tempo rubato* is a deliberate substitution of other note values for those that have been notated in the score. The duration values in Fig. 59, on the contrary, are arrived at within tolerances that prevent confusion with the next closest possible note values. For one performance, they *are* the note values of the score according to decisions made in terms of their functions for the structure.

Throughout the distribution of durations as well as the establishment of levels of salience, the performer has been aware of the entire course of the main melody in this *Minore* section. He attributes its somber, melancholy context to a certain rise and fall of the melody in graduated, scalewise steps combined with a tendency to burst out in *sforzandi* and reach strong climaxes only to subside in the drooping phrases of the coda. This total design of the melody turns the constant triplet motion of the pattern of asynchronization into a supplement or background that can provide either a roaring buildup for the climaxes or a rumbling subsidence for the decline into *pianissimos*. The triplets also contribute an undercurrent of agitation during the softer measures and a dramatic power during the stronger. Yet without their rhythmic and melodic redundancy, they would not be available for these contextual purposes.

Indeed, the justification of contextual purposes must come from the evidence of redundancy, not simply from an outside reference even when it is authenticated by the composer. To enlarge on this particular point, let us consider the first movement of Beethoven's Piano Sonata No. 27 in E minor, Op. 90, the opening theme of which is stated in Fig. 60(a). For Schindler, who acted as a sort of secretary or amanuensis to the composer, stated that Beethoven had given it the subtitle "Struggle Between Head and Heart."[50] Count Moritz von Lichnowsky, to whom the Sonata is dedicated, and his brother, Count Carl von Lichnowsky, were devoted patrons of Beethoven. At the time, Count Moritz was facing the problem of whether to marry beneath his station, the object of his love being Fräulein Stummer, a Viennese singer. He eventually did marry her, but meanwhile he struggled between the dictates of caution and the impulses of passion, a dilemma that intrigued Beethoven, who had himself struggled over desires to marry.

The dramatic use of strong contrasts is a well-known feature of Beethoven's music. Consequently, whether or not Lichnowsky's situation figured in his incentives to compose Op. 90, the contrast it embodied was made to order for the composer's structural methods. He could place in close opposition measures designed to convey violent force and measures designed to

FIG. 60
Piano Sonata No. 27 in E minor, Op. 90, by Beethoven

(a)
Mit Lebhaftigkeit und durchaus mit Empfindung und Ausdruck

convey moderation and control. Our interest is in whether such objectives are reflected in the composer's management of foreground redundancy. The first thing we notice is the rhythmic redundancy of two-measure links, Fig. 60(b). As a result, the rhythmic pattern will become a continuing stimulus and the detection of differences from link to link will shift from rhythmic to other clues. Next, we see that the harmony within each measure is a unit, due to the passing tones in measures 1 and 5 and the neighboring or returning tones in measures 3 and 7. This circumstance reduces the background to the rising succession of chords in Fig. 60(c). Two factors, then, the repetitiveness of the rhythm and the arrangement of the background in harmonic units, produce the organic redundancy by means of which we detect the sequential nature of the continuity.

We are now in a position to compare link I (measures 1 and 2) with link II (measures 3 and 4) for differences. We see that within the harmonic redundancy that characterizes both links, in link I only the soprano part has melodic motion whereas in link II all the parts move contrapuntally, particularly the bass, which is in contrary motion to the soprano. Likewise, the melodic movement in link I seems abrupt whereas that of link II seems smooth. The reason for this difference becomes clear with the aid of the background progression in Fig. 60(c). The connection of the chords is more remote in link I than in link II. That is, although the opening chord in link I states the E minor key of the movement, it is in reality used by Beethoven as the submediant of G major, and progression from the submediant to the dominant is a notably abrupt one. Its abruptness becomes all the more evident from the contrast with link II, which progresses smoothly from the dominant to the tonic of G major. We also notice the disjunct motion of the soprano in link I, which skips from the E on the third quarter of measure 1 up to A in measure 2, whereas the analogous note in link II, the A on the third quarter of measure 3, moves smoothly and stepwise to B in measure 4.

This entire process is repeated sequentially between links III and IV during measures 5 through 8. In measure 5, the tonic chord takes on the guise of the submediant in B minor so that the same progress to the dominant and the tonic of this minor key may be achieved. Whether the motion from a G major chord to an F-sharp major chord is viewed in this fashion or as progress that is still in G major from the tonic to the dominant of the mediant, we are dealing with a very abrupt connection of chords. Indeed, the progression in link III is even more abrupt than that in link I because the skip in the soprano becomes an augmented fourth or tritone.

Pursuing Beethoven's methods of contrast further, we observe that he has placed eighth rests in links I and III as opposed to the *portamento* indications (*staccato* dots below a curve) in links II and IV. The duration of these eighth rests or silences, at a tempo of 160 strokes per minute for quarter notes, would be roughly 19/100ths of a second. Some editions, in links I and III, add *staccato* dots to the upbeats. However, Beethoven has shown by the fullness of his harmonization in these links that he wishes their heaviness to contrast with the lightness of links II and IV (he has marked the links alternately *forte* and *piano*). Consequently, these editions are in error, and the tolerances for the upbeat chords should be larger rather than smaller. The tolerances for the following rests then become correspondingly smaller, suggesting such a relationship as 22/100ths of a second for the duration of the upbeat chord to 16/100ths of a second for that of the following rest.

As to the *portamento* dots below curves in links II and IV, the needs of contrast dictate that the moment of silence between upbeat and downbeat be very short. Indeed, we wonder why Beethoven did not connect these beats with a complete *legato* until we realize that he was reserving *legato* for the phrase that begins in measure 9. Since each quarter could receive a duration of about 38/100ths of a second at the tempo of 160 strokes, the duration of these *portamento* chords could easily be above 30/100ths of a second.

In the meantime, the rhythmic and harmonic evolutionary redundancy of links I and III has indicated salience for the soprano part. The soprano still dominates in links II and IV but for a different reason. There, the redundancy is organic rhythmically, and this renders the contrapuntal motion of the parts evident. Ordinarily, contrapuntal motion would reduce the salience of any one part, but the previous disjunct melodic line of links I and III acts to center attention on the conjunct soprano of links II and IV. Also, the alto and tenor parts of links II and IV are more static, and only the bass, which is in contrary motion with the soprano, could receive a measure of salience.

On the whole, the tolerances for links I and III should be smaller than for those governing links II and IV. This difference is generally required wherever a rhythmic impression is desired in contrast to a melodic, and here, too, the rhythmic redundancy of links II and IV reduces the articulation that links I and III need. However, playing links II and IV at a slower tempo than links I and III in order to increase the contrast is in the same doubtful category as *tempo rubato*. The composer, as we have shown, has himself provided the requisite basis for contrast from link to link.

Accordingly, Beethoven succeeds in achieving a relationship of contrast between a forceful, violent link and a moderated, controlled link. It is ridiculous that anyone hearing this theme would immediately think "Of course, this is Count Lichnowsky's dilemma about marrying." But the human characteristics that are present when a person's attitude is impulsive as opposed to reasoned are analogous to the musical characteristics that Beethoven has presented and contrasted in his links. An impulsive person is abrupt, noisy, sharp. A reasoned individual is quiet and controlled and his thoughts are clearly related. The important point is that the music and its subtitle be congruous in this manner, not that one should suggest the other. Thus, we could perceive no analogy if Count Lichnowsky were said to be marching in a parade or attending a funeral. The test of a

composer or a performer is not how vividly he has suggested a
scene or a situation but how perceptively he has grouped
characteristics that in human experience are appropriate to
one another.

32 THE PERFORMER AND THE LISTENER

As the listener is thus helped to derive the relationships from
link to link in the continuity of a composition, his status is not
unlike that of a person who reads a play and later attends a
performance of it. To read a play is to obtain an idea of its
scenes, characters, and plot and to discern its meaning. But
whatever one receives from reading the play cannot compare
with its impact in full production, with actors speaking and
acting out their parts. For each of the actors has made decisions
that are related to the total meaning of the play, decisions about
the timing of his speech, the tone of his voice, and accompanying
gestures and movements. Similarly, the musical performer
makes an immense number of decisions all of which are designed
to bring out the central purpose of the composition. His results
are attributable not simply to the actuality of tone color or
duration or accent but to his selection of performance values
that in his opinion reveal the total objective of the music.

Let us then summarize his effort, which is essentially concerned with many different forms of *calculation*. He begins by
calculating the evolutionary redundancy of the first link in the
given continuity. This is the overdetermination of harmonic,
rhythmic, and melodic elements from which he can estimate
their contribution to the foreground. On the basis of their
contribution, he can discover the more remote relationships
that point at once to the design of the passage and its salient
characteristics.

Then the calculations change from imagined to physically
real ones. The salience of characteristics is to be achieved in
terms of saliences among tones. Which tones have natural

salience? Which tones will tend toward salience as a result of location in the structure, of the order in which they occur, of their relative dissonance and consonance? By calculating and achieving degrees of salience among the tones, the performer turns the relationships that redundancy has made evident to him into the salient characteristics of the passage.

With the arrival of the second link in the continuity, there is a return to imagined calculations, this time in terms of organic redundancy. How much does the second link resemble the first? What are the precise differences between them and what is their purpose? Has the composer altered the evolutionary complexity of the second link? The answers to these questions decide what should be salient in the second link and provide the basis for calculating its performance values. Those elements that become continuing stimuli will no longer need the more restricted tolerances they had in the first link. The tolerances can be larger provided that no confusion is created with the adjacent possibilities in the hierarchies that natural salience has set up. Thus enlarged, the tolerances permit a wider choice of performance values and make them available for the further purposes of salience in the second link. Despite the enlargement, the materials that are similar in both links will seem unchanged to the listener. He has been helped to a new experience of salience in the second link without disturbing his recollection of the first.

As far as the composer is concerned, any doubts he may have about the listener's ability to accomplish the required acts of comparison between adjacent links are mitigated by his decision to write for *the* listener as opposed to *a* listener. But from the listener's point of view, the task of comparing links has been eased considerably by the intervention of the performer. The performer does all the work of calculation and presents links that have already been compared. In short, the listener is relieved of originating or organizing the comparison, but he must know how to listen in order to catch its details. Like so many other and familiar situations in which the individual is aware of what needs to be done, judges the outcome, but turns over the actual work to someone else, the listening situation requires the hearer to discern the links and to draw conclusions from the performer's comparison of them but not to go through the calculations that obtained that comparison.

Obviously, there is a profusion of situations in modern life when someone else must do the actual work. No one person can be expected to have the knowledge and the training to meet them all. However, where the individual turns over the actual work with only a faint inkling of what is needed and with poor judgment of the outcome, the standard of the actual work will inevitably fall. It is the function of education to prevent this fall to low standards, to see to it that individuals are aware of what goes into the actual work and that they are capable of judging the outcome. In carrying out this function, education has no alternative to assuming that individuals have the basic ability to reach these objectives. Thus in the case of music, to err on the side of overestimating the capacity of listeners is beneficial. It demonstrates what listening should be even if in many instances the desired conditions are not yet available. To hold out an ideal will eventually create more listeners who can uphold it, whereas catering to low capacity cuts off all hope of improvement.

With the insight we have gained into the performer's activity, it is easy to see of what such catering to low capacity, such playing down to the listener, consists. We have shown that the presence of redundancy is the signal to seek more remote relationships among the foreground elements. The performer who plays to the gallery, on the contrary, emphasizes the redundancy at the expense of the more remote relationships. For example, Chopin's Etude in A-flat major, Op. 25, No. 1, Fig. 61(a), exhibits a high degree of rhythmic and harmonic redundancy in both organic and evolutionary respects. The initial link of two measures already contains seven repetitions of the pattern of asynchronization and the succeeding links are constructed in the same way. The remote relationships, therefore, are in the course of the soprano melody, in synthetic timbre, in implied motions of voice-leading, and in certain harmonic changes that occur in the background progression.

To dazzle his auditors, then, this performer sidesteps the redundant aspect of the Etude and emphasizes the rhythmic and melodic characteristics of the patterns of asynchronization themselves. He prevents these patterns from becoming a continuing stimulus and turns them into a *continual* stimulus. They

FIG. 61

Etude in A-flat major, Op. 25, No. 1, by Chopin

obtrude into the listener's consciousness, thwarting his natural ability to relegate their rhythm and outline to subconscious awareness. This insistent hammering thus has the effect of shifting the listener's attention away from the music and to the skill of the performer in traversing the patterns at high speed. The same treatment of the Etude's concluding bars, Fig. 61(b), only reinforces the substitution of admiring the performer for deriving the music's meaning. Here, what is merely an after-thought of a prevailing tone color is turned into a pyro-technical display of parallel arpeggios for both hands.

This explanation of the mechanics of display serves to dis-tinguish the conscientious performers from the exploiters. The conscientious performer uses redundancy as a stepping-stone to the salience of remote structural objectives. The exploiter manipulates redundancy in order to be admired. The effect of conscientious performance, therefore, is to efface the performer. His skill is hidden by the continual appearance of saliences that keep the listener's attention on the musical continuity instead of drawing it to himself. Indeed, such a performer is dis-appointed when the listener's reaction is to his muscular skill. Having put so much effort into the creation and linkage of saliences and knowing how easy it is to exploit redundancy, he resents being classed with those who lower the art of perform-ance to the level of an exhibition.

To help him sustain this attitude, the conscientious performer finds a model in the conscientious composer. For in composing, too, it is possible to exploit redundancy to show off structural skills. The ideal of conscientious composition is to create the illusion of independent existence for the composition. That is, it should seem to stand by itself rather than need propping by the composer in the form of supplementary explanations. Music gives the illusion of independence when it is to the greatest possible extent self-explanatory, when the natural salience of its materials combines with an expertly managed rate of change from link to link to focus the listener's attention on the con-tinuity and away from the man who devised it. The conscientious composer, too, experiences a sense of failure when the listener reacts to his skill instead of to the expressive purpose of the music. At one extreme, he fears that his composition may seem "sicklied o'er with the pale cast of thought" and, at the other, that it may become a "war horse" for the exhibitionist performer. For him, artistic success is greatest when he and the listener have exchanged positions of remoteness. As the listener is drawn closely to the music, the composer seems remote from it. That is, the more engrossed the listener, the greater the concealment of the composer's work and, accordingly, the greater the independence of the composition.

To complete the roster of the conscientious, there are listeners, too, who are equally concerned for the well-being of the art. Without knowing the mechanics we have explained or the terms we have used, they can detect when either the performer or the composer is misusing foreground redundancy for the purposes of display. They are not drawn to the concert hall by extravagant publicity that holds out the bait of "sensational" performance or music of "unprecedented novelty." They are repelled by promises of a "sensational performance" of Beethoven's sonatas or Bach's preludes and fugues. Such listeners realize that to understand music requires effort, just as performance and composition do, and that it becomes easier with practice. One must learn to absorb music in links and to compare them in depth and in succession. Also, one must become conversant with idiom and sensitive to contexts. Then the circle of that remoteness which is the criterion of artistic success is complete. The performance conceals the performer from the listener; the score seems to express without the presence of the composer; the listener has been drawn into contact with the expressive meaning of the music, and his remoteness either through lack of interest or through disbelief has been overcome.

VI THE DEFINITION OF MUSICAL TALENT

33 CONVERSANCE WITH IDIOM

In this chapter we shall define musical talent in terms of the principles that have been set forth in the preceding chapters. In following this order, in deciding what an activity is before estimating the qualities it requires, we shall be more logical than the approaches that attempt to define talent without relating it to goals in artistic expression. Their faults have arisen not from the measurements, experiments, or questionnaires, which are often both ingenious and painstaking, but from the doubts whether what has been measured is indeed an attribute of musical talent. The controversies have not been over the investigations but over the conclusions drawn from them, and, while these arguments go on, it is not entirely fair to the student to make him undergo tests for musical aptitude. In most instances, he is accepting a judgment upon his musical ability without knowing that there is considerable difference of opinion about what musical talent is.[51] We shall be careful, therefore, to avoid this situation and to relate a particular need for talent to a specific objective in performance.

First and foremost, the student of performance must be conversant with idiom, and some students acquire this conversance more easily than others. Let us review what we have said about conversance with idiom and add to it in the light of the subject of talent. We shall again use the parallel with language because the oral supplement to the score, where the idioms of music are to be found, has the same function in music as dictionaries and books on usage have in language.

Thus, there are accepted connotations for musical motifs and accepted ways of using them in phrases just as there are accepted meanings for words and accepted usages when employing them in sentences. These connotations and usages constitute an idiom that belongs to its time and depends upon the prevailing practice of the musicians of that time. By their musical pronunciation, they establish the levels of prosaic and poetic salience. They select musical materials on the basis of natural salience and settle upon the tolerances which surround that salience. They can either exert or resist pressure on these ranges of the tolerance and thereby affect the adoption of new ranges that signify a change in pronunciation. In language, a good example of the pressure of pronunciations is the word "glister," which became archaic and gave way to "glitter." The tolerances governing the pronunciation of "glister" became so wide or even indeterminate in range that it was replaced by "glitter," which then became the new natural salience. Similarly, early recordings show us to what an extent musical pronunciation has changed in a relatively short time. In general, tempi are now stricter and contrasts are less striking.

Since the student absorbs the prevailing musical pronunciation during childhood, the conditions affecting his musical speech, which depend on his family and his teachers, should be carefully controlled. First, they must explain to him the vital difference between the legitimate, eventual changes that the pressures on pronunciation and usage bring about and the illegitimate changes that are threatened by mispronunciation and misusage. When a speaker says "tweny" instead of "twenty," he is mispronouncing, not exerting the legitimate pressure of speech on language, because he has omitted a root component of the word. In "twenty," the suffix "ty" represents the root, "tens," which gives the word its significance: two tens. Modifying "ty" into "y" would require change of all the words in the same category: "thiry" instead of "thirty," "fory" instead of "forty." In the case of usage, too, the speaker who uses the word "disinterested" in the sense of "uninterested" has deprived the language of a distinction between avoiding a conflict of interest and not being interested at all.

Musical speech, too, has its mispronunciations and misusages. Fig. 62 is an excerpt from Chopin's Waltz No. 11 in

FIG. 62
Waltz No. 11 in G-flat major, Op. 60, No. 1, by Chopin

G-flat major, Op. 70, No. 1. At (a) is the actual notation; (b) shows the mispronunciation. The brackets that have been added to (a) and (b) explain why the music must be pronounced as Chopin wrote it. The eighth note and dotted eighth note resolve the dissonance on the downbeat; to turn the eighth note into a sixteenth note is to change its purpose from resolution into a rhythmic preparation of the next measure. The consonant downbeats of the next section, (c), have possibly encouraged this mispronunciation, which leaves the dissonances dangling.

Musical misusages usually result from choosing an inadvisable place for the strongest accent in the phrase. In Fig. 63, the opening measures of Chopin's Nocturne in F-sharp major, Op. 15, No. 2, the main accent is often misplaced on the third eighth of the second measure (marked *) and usually with a *crescendo* on the preceding thirty-second notes. The main accent belongs on the downbeat of measure 1, and the thirty-second notes and third eighth note of measure 2 have a purely decorative purpose.

In addition to protecting the child's musical pronunciation and usage, his parents and teachers also have the responsibility of acquainting him with the idioms of earlier epochs. For example, without their intervention he would remain unaware of certain features that characterize the phrases of Mozart's

FIG. 63
Nocturne in F-sharp major, Op. 15, No. 2, by Chopin

time, such as the so-called *feminine* endings. Feminine endings are analogous to the heavy-light pattern of trochees that have a very light second syllable, as in the word "sofa," as opposed to "window." In Fig. 64(a), from the second movement of Mozart's Piano Sonata in F major, K.280, they are marked with asterisks. The eighth notes at the end of the curves must be extremely light. There is no hint of this requirement in the notation although, as Fig. 64(b) shows, Mozart sometimes sets the precedent for it in such works as the Piano Sonata in G major, K.283, where the duration of the second component in the trocheelike pattern is reduced by rests. Features like these are part of the oral supplement to the score during the second half of the 18th century. The student can learn about them only from his teacher, who explains them as details of an attitude toward ornamentation maintained by an epoch that was highly committed to grace, refinement, and the importance of manner.

The responsibility shared by family and teachers to familiarize the student with existing and earlier idioms can easily fall short of its goal unless it is guided by two major educational influences, namely, the canons of taste and the discipline of research. By *taste* we mean the preservation of standards from

Fig. 64

(a) Second movement, Piano Sonata in F major, K.280, by Mozart

(b) Second movement, Piano Sonata in G major, K.283, by Mozart

carelessness or indifference, as in the insistence upon "twenty" instead of "tweny" or upon the eighth note in Fig. 62(a) instead of the sixteenth note in (b). By *research* we mean the recovery of a bygone, oral supplement to the score, as in the case of features of Mozart's idiom. With these two influences in force, any dangers that are inherent in imitation, which is the main avenue to pronunciation, are overcome. Taste and research provide the necessary safeguards against either debasement or ignorance during learning by imitation.

Yet imitative or rote methods should not be subjected to

undue criticism. Indeed, as an instrument of learning, imitation is both powerful and effective, and the possibility of an element of slavishness in it for which it is often criticized arises more from what is being imitated than from imitation itself. We are apt to underestimate its value because we tend to overlook the new difference offered by the person who is imitating and see only the old sameness offered by the model. Each new person brings a somewhat different roster of qualities to the act of imitating which prevents the outcome from ever being precisely the same. In this circumstance lies the efficacy of the range of fluctuation within the tolerance. And the existence of the tolerance brings into play an ability that is definitely an ingredient of talent, namely, the ability to obtain any performance value within the tolerance *at will*.

The nature of this ingredient of talent is clarified by the distinction between a person with a pronounced ability to imitate and one who merely imitates, a distinction that depends on the difference between conscious and unconscious activity. The people we cited, who clap in unison at a game, have unconsciously measured a duration and created similar ones. This ability is both considerable and of great value, but it is limited by the need for and presence of a model duration that is to be duplicated. The musician, on the contrary, must be able to create the model, to measure duration consciously. He must find the duration value that he desires within the range offered by the tolerance. He is like an actor who can reproduce the tone and inflection of another person's speech by detecting the values within the tolerance that that person habitually employs. Like the actor, too, his method depends upon a certain amount of trial and error—that is, it includes the possibility of modifying the duration values until the desired one appears. Thus, memory for the achieved value, once it has appeared, is an important component of the talent to create performance values at will. Memory acts to retain the results of the process whereby what is conducive to similarity is preserved and what is alien is rejected.

For the musician, then, conversance with idiom is a consciously available resource and he can call upon it ultimately with great ease and flexibility. He can shift almost automatically from the idiom of Mozart to that of Brahms, from the contrasts of Beethoven to the tone color of Debussy. The combined influences of taste and research help him to keep the distinctions between idioms clear and to associate particular sets of tolerances with each. Research enables him to differentiate between *staccato* in Haydn's music and *staccato* in Debussy's, and taste confirms his belief that he has found appropriate values for each. The effect is reciprocal: Research prevents taste from being purely whimsical, and taste prevents research from inducing literalness or pedantry.

34 SENSITIVITY TO CONTEXT

Yet the very term, *idiom*, reminds us that we must add something further to the sheer talent for imitation. "Idiom" implies a certain generality, whereas "imitation" is local and limited to the particular. To explain this distinction, we can again find no better instance than the art of acting. For the actor regards his ability to startle and amuse us with mimicry as a side issue of his art. It is a chip from a block that he is shaping for a further purpose. He took his first steps, perhaps by mimicking well-known personages. But soon he was able to generalize about the salient characteristics he had discovered. The voices of aged people seemed to share certain features, those of the young, other ones; in happiness, people spoke in one way, in grief, in another. For this reason, and rightly, the actor came to consider the creation of the imaginary characters in a play a higher form of art than mimicry is. It implies a more subtle form of observation and of reproduction. It has the wider application lent by the universality of shared experience. The earlier purpose, the purpose of mimicry, was to make the spectator recognize the well-known personage. Now, in the higher form, the purpose was to make the spectator recognize his own behavioural traits in the personages of the play. The mimicry of mankind in general replaced the mimicry of a particular person.

Using our own terms to describe this progress from the particular to the general, we can say that universal contexts were found for individual performance values. A certain performance value lost attachment to one particular individual because all people were observed to gravitate toward it in similar situations. Thus, we know that people's voices tend to rise in pitch when they are excited or that the tempo of their speech will slow down when they are conveying serious or portentous meanings. The infinite varieties of human experience may be grouped under a limited number of headings and related to clusters of qualities that belong together because they are mutually appropriate. The talent that must be added to the ability to mimic, therefore, is a sensitivity to the context of human experience and to the clusters of qualities that are appropriate to them.

Ordinarily, this sensitivity to salient human characteristics is called *poetic* talent. It becomes musical only when the perception of appropriateness is centered in the phenomena of sound and hearing. This distinction remains in force even when both poetry and music invoke the same contexts, as in the case of songs. They are separate media even though it is possible to speak of a musical quality in poetry and of a poetic quality in music. Their separation is proven by the hesitancy of most musicians with the materials of poetry. Of course, there are exceptions, but these are rare. Schumann, for example, was equally sensitive to the contexts of music and poetry, and this access to both media was undoubtedly responsible for the unique excellence of his songs. John Dowland, the Elizabethan composer who set his own poetry to music, is another striking example. But from the point of view of performance, what we value most in Schumann's double endowment was his felicity in describing the contexts of music poetically. Any musician who can describe musical contexts in poetic terms, even if he cannot approach the prowess of Schumann, possesses a decided interpretive advantage.

Among recent performers, Cortot stands out in the ability to summon the powers of poetry for the description of musical contexts. Of Ravel's *Le Gibet* (from *Gaspard de la nuit*), which was composed under the influence of Aloysius Bertrand's somber evocation of the scene of a hanging, Cortot wrote: "The indefinable mystery of chords that trail in the shadowy gloom of dissonances and ghostly resolutions is combined with an atmosphere of terror which a muted sonority or prevailing pianissimo sustains throughout the composition, giving way to a mezzo forte only once and then for but three measures. All the elements that inspire fear seem to have been exploited here, with a surpassing discernment and an incomparable ingenuity for macabre effect." [52] As we have already noted, the value of this type of poetic description for the performer is that it keeps the continuity of the music in view. There is a notable balance between references to aspects of the context and references to components of the musical structure. If in some instances the mixture is very rich and the adjectives and nouns seem to overflow the sentences, that very profusion, when they are well chosen, will stimulate the performer to search more deeply for the appropriate musical sonority and for the exactly right adjustment of tempo. The performer who submits his search for performance values to the influence of relevant, evocative words will achieve *greater selectivity* within the ranges of the tolerance.

Two areas that are highly susceptible to poetic influence are those of synthetic and thematic timbre. Concerning an example of synthetic timbre discussed earlier, Brahms' Ballade in D minor, Op. 10, No. 1 (Fig. 54), we can now point out that its tones were arranged to produce a timbre that would be appropriate to the poetic context. The composer has indicated, in the subtitle *Edward*, that he is here setting the opening question of the *Edward Ballade* (it is included in Percy's *Reliques of English*

Poetry) : "O why does your sword so drop with blood, Edward, Edward?" Brahms has not only been faithful to the syllabic structure but has composed the melody in true ballad style. Therefore, the student who can imagine how such a line would be sung, indeed, how such a question would be spoken, is in a better position to obtain the most appropriate synthetic timbre. Edward's evasive answers to his mother's questions, his ultimate confession, his curse of a mother who has conspired with him to kill his father—these elements of the ballad conjure up an atmosphere of tragic drama that greatly stimulates the search for appropriate performance values. Again, the listener will not derive the story of Edward from the performance. But he

FIG. 65
Second movement, Piano Sonata No. 17 in D minor, Op. 31, No. 2, by Beethoven

will undergo the stimuli of qualities that approach nearer to the ones that the composer, in view of his subtitle, must have wished. When the performance has not been based on these circumstances governing the composition, the listener will also be stimulated but in ways that belie the composer's effort.

The same considerations apply to thematic timbre. In Fig. 65, from Beethoven's Piano Sonata No. 17 in D minor, Op. 31, No. 2, the student has a better chance of finding appropriate values if he is aware that, in this as well as in numerous other slow movements for piano, the composer thought in orchestral terms, almost as if he were transcribing an orchestral score for keyboard. The reference to horns and tympani in this excerpt is unmistakable. By imagining the sounds of these instruments, the performer discovers appropriate tone color for the chords and appropriate rhythmic inflection for the *gruppetti* in the bass. Naturally, the effect is not the same as with actual horns and tympani. But we must remember that when a composer orchestrates, he seeks among a number of instruments the one most capable of producing the expressive effect he has in mind. The instrument he chooses must still be considered secondary to the effect he desires because only in his opinion is it the best for his purpose and because the player, due to lack of skill or other reasons, may fail to carry out his wishes. Similarly, the pianist's success should not be measured by how well he imitates horns and tympani but by how well he succeeded in creating the effect those instruments were expected to achieve. The orchestrator has a great potential advantage in the large roster of instruments at his disposal, but, judged from the point of view of effects actually created, the pianist is not at as great a disadvantage as might at first be supposed.

Synthetic timbre and thematic timbre, then, illustrate the value of poetic influence to performance. But poetry rightfully affects every other resource of performance. It motivates, for example, the choice of duration values for such rhythmic patterns as the dotted eighth note and sixteenth note. This pattern is basic to the rhythm of the mazurka. Chopin wrote more than fifty mazurkas and perhaps five or six do not contain it. Yet the adherence to the same rhythmic pattern does not mean that all mazurkas are alike in mood. When they are described poetically, such adjectives as "melancholy," "whimsical," "national," and "waltzlike" are frequently used, and the variety of adjectives points to differences of spirit among them. In performance, the burden of making these differences clear is carried by the rhythmic pattern, and therefore this pattern cannot always mean the same thing despite the fact that it is notated in the same way.

Despite the identical notation, the significance of the dotted eighth and sixteenth-note pattern alters with the changes in poetic context. The performer must respond to this situation by choosing different values within the tolerance. Thus, shortening the duration of the sixteenth note will contribute to lightness or whimsicality of expression; lengthening it will make the pattern more suited to sober or pathetic expression. Due to the phenomenon of the tolerance, such shortening or lengthening of the sixteenth note does not affect the listener's perception of one and the same rhythmic pattern in both instances. Nor will he know that different poetic descriptions of the context prompted the performer's choice. The listener will simply accept the service of the rhythmic pattern to the prevailing mood of the piece brought out in the performance.

35 MUSCULAR ABILITIES

Some students are naturally endowed for the muscular aspect of performance just as some people are better equipped, physically, for athletics. Yet due to two circumstances, the need for muscular talent is often misjudged. First, performance is presented after an anterior period of preparation. It is therefore difficult to judge how much of the proficiency in the performance was acquired by practice and how much was due to natural or initial ability. To most observers, the work during the practice sessions remains hidden, and they ascribe the results to innate skill. Second, the less experienced among listeners, not being orientated toward deriving the expressive content of the performance, receive the full impact of its muscular skill. They are not yet taken up in the purpose of musical expression, and, shorn of purpose, the activity of performance seems but an adventure in dexterity. They are still in the class of people to whom engraving a religious motto on the head of a pin seems a greater feat of skill than repairing a watch.

As a result of these two factors that affect the judgment, many people think of muscular abilities when they think about musical talent. When their children rebel against continuing music lessons, they believe the cause to be discouragement over lack of muscular ability. Actually, the potential of the average hand is more than adequate for a large number of the muscular tasks in performance. The fault lies rather in a teaching method that disregards this potential and enforces one uniform approach to muscular control that all hands must adopt whatever their differences in size, shape, and muscular tendency. All are pressed into the mold of reigning beliefs about hand position and finger action instead of taking advantage of natural muscular inclinations; and were a more pragmatic attitude toward the powers of hands to be adopted, there would be much greater confidence among students concerning muscular matters and more individuality as well. The classic example of rigidity in method is the rejection of Chopin's potential by Kalkbrenner, a noted pianist and teacher of the time, which almost deprived the world of a new pianistic style.[53]

Judgments about muscular ability cannot be made, too, without first having clear ideas about the nature of performance. There is a tendency to plunge into the work of playing, to place the music on the stand and begin, without acquainting the student with principles that are to govern the activity. Without this kind of briefing about the place and the purpose of his instrumental study, the student lapses into the idea that he is to pit his proficiency against the criticism of the audience, and he cannot help viewing this proficiency as chiefly muscular. He is thus slanted toward overcoming—toward overcoming his competitors in a struggle for the favor of the audience. He will either be victorious or go down in defeat. While there is nothing wrong in being ambitious, the battle we are describing goes on outside the composition. Instead of dealing with the problems of expression within it, the student, in his practice sessions, arms himself against possible defeat. He is ridden with anxiety during this time of preparation and overdoes or overplays when he should be planning or analyzing. He is impelled to dogged repetition when he should be clarifying the immediate aims of practicing. It was to counteract these tendencies that Walter Gieseking and his teacher, Karl Leimer, proposed a method of learning compositions away from the instrument and before a note is played.[54]

Once the student takes a more reasonable attitude toward the need for muscular skill he will stop struggling to acquire more and more muscular abilities and instead adapt ones he already has. Instead of trying to match a facility that others are said to possess, he will make use of his own muscular inclinations to carry out defined needs of performance. Under this changed attitude, he would first relate muscular energy to the multilayered construction of the foreground, allotting the larger motions to the basic layers and the smaller motions to the surface layers. The steps based on layer analysis, which we described in the synthesis of method, would take care of the integration of large and small motions so that they can occur simultaneously or coincidentally. Following the correct order of the layers from the background to the foreground enables a hierarchy of large to small motions to come about naturally in terms of the potential of the hand.

Then the student would adapt muscular energy to the purposes of salience. This requirement, which concerns every phase of performance, may be illustrated here on a small scale by Fig. 66, an excerpt from Brahms's Rhapsody in G minor, Op. 79, No. 2. The most salient element is the melody in the bass staff of measures 3 and 4 because it is the echo of the treble melody in measures 1 and 2. However, the B natural in measure 3, which begins the echo, is enclosed within the chord for the right hand, as the bracket shows. This disadvantageous location for salience is overcome by fingering the chord as shown in Fig. 66, namely, 412 instead of 421. Now the thumb, the heaviest finger of the hand, plays the B natural. Its muscular potential has been adapted to a need for salience.

Similar adaptations for the varied purposes of performance as a whole depend not only on touch but on two forms of hearing, inner and actual. Inner hearing, which is coincident with silent reading, imagines the saliences of the score in terms of the composer's manipulation of foreground redundancy.

Actual hearing is concerned with the local conditions of physical salience, that is, which tones are naturally salient and which will need adjustment for salience. Touch comes into play and its necessities are decided only after the results of inner hearing are compared with the results of actual hearing. As we have said, these decisions about touch should then be carried out in terms

FIG. 66
Rhapsody in G minor, Op. 79, No. 2, by Brahms

of the natural, muscular inclination so that the required saliences are achieved by motions that are best suited both to them and to the potential of the hand.

The fact that inner and actual hearing supervise the operations of touch has an important bearing upon the judgment of muscular talent. Since good performance depends upon adjusting touch to the needs of salience, its excellence may have owed as much to discerning choice of saliences as to proper adaptations of touch. A student's muscular talent, then, cannot be judged per se but should be estimated in terms of general, yet pertinent resources. He must have suppleness and flexibility of the hand, wrist, and arm in order to permit the integration of large and small motions; he must have the co-ordination that allows one of these three components momentarily to dominate the others and thereby produce variations in touch. To these resources must be added a tenacious memory both for sounds and for the motions that produced them. The motions, singly and in combination, the saliences, the touches for the saliences, must all be remembered. Otherwise, consistency in performance is impossible. The effort that has assigned a specific interpretive objective to each passage will be wasted.

Finally, the student is required to adapt muscular energy so that a sense of continuousness in the music may be derived, so that the rhythmic, chain-link construction of the musical continuity is served. All the touch formations and the saliences they achieve are to be produced while the hand, wrist, and arm are in motion and within links that are designed according to rhythmic principles. Fortunately, this requirement is not as arduous as it sounds because there is a built-in relation between rhythm and motion: It is easier to carry out and remember muscular motions when they are done rhythmically, as work songs like the *Volga Boat Song* attest. Yet the student must be careful to distinguish between motion that is merely rhythmic in itself, and therefore sheer facility, and motion that serves the rhythm of the continuity in terms of required saliences. For this reason, etudes are more useful to him than purely muscular exercises. Etudes conform to the chain-link construction of music. While their organic redundancy from link to link is usually too great to produce good music, their well-defined rhythm helps to develop the touch-on-the-wing that performance demands.

36 Interest in Musical Analysis

Until very recently, musicians were interchangeably composers and performers. Indeed, Bach, during his lifetime, was better known as an organist than as a composer, and Mozart and Beethoven customarily gave the first performance of their piano concerti. Yet despite such figures as Rachmaninov and Prokofiev, who were exemplifying this interchangeability in the present century, the idea that the student trains differently for performance and for composition has gained widespread acceptance. It has become so entrenched that we must now speak of interesting the student of performance in musical analysis, an area of study that leads into composition and that was once considered essential for every musician. There is a natural flair for musical analysis just as there is a type of mind that delights in taking things apart and in finding reasons for their construction. But due to the circumstances that have separated the performer from the composer, we are forced to convince students of the value of analysis and to promote their "interest in" it before we can judge their "talent for" it.

The incongruity of this situation is all the greater because, undoubtedly, the best way to learn how to perform is to compose. Everyone who can compose is not automatically a good performer. But since knowledge of musical structure is essential for performance and the most direct and efficient way of acquiring that knowledge is by composing, the study of composition should be requisite for all performers. The study of harmony, counterpoint, and form is not enough because they are most often presented to performers as subjects in themselves and in a way that is not synonymous with composition. Although composition utilizes features that may be studied under these three headings, it is above and beyond them. Like performance, it is an act. It consists in carrying out, in manipulating materials, whereas harmony, counterpoint, and form do not exist independently. They are concomitants and are achieved each time that a composition is written. That is why we find Schubert's intention to study counterpoint, which he is said to have formed shortly before he died, so paradoxical. We wonder who would have dared to teach him.

Conversely, learning to compose will not automatically make the performer a good composer. Rather it will help him with the all-important tasks of separating musical continuity into links and of comparing them for foreground redundancy. He will move more easily among the layers that are super-imposed on the background. He will find it easier to sketch, because sketching means, in reality, to play the composition in terms of the background or intermediate layers rather than only in terms of the foreground. His approach to the foreground will be improvisatory, more like that of the composer in the first stages of creating the music, and he will therefore have a wider field of choice for performance values. In essence, he will be recapitulating the composer's steps in writing the music and will thus have a better chance of finding an appropriate interpretation.

All evidence points to the conclusion that performance and composition are reverse sides of the same coin. There should be no hesitation, then, about turning either side of the coin face upward. For a misguided awe of composition has resulted from separating it for special study by selected individuals, and if one starts early enough this disadvantage can be overcome.[55] Otherwise, we will stand by and watch the frustration of the urge to compose lead young students to the field of popular music. These students are undoubtedly attracted by the freedom to play popular music in other ways than the one that has been notated and to improvise variations on a given framework. The improvisatory approach to the performance of masterpieces of the past, which we have just described, will check this exodus to the popular field. While it differs from the approach of popular music in not permitting the final stage of performance to differ from the score, its reliance on sketching during the earlier stages offers the requisite freedom to improvise.

We can be sure, too, that the forbidding emphasis on accuracy per se has caused students to desert the music of the past. Such emphasis places a premium on skill before the student has the chance to become conversant with the materials of the composition and with its aims in expression. The compositional approach, the opportunity to sketch, provides a stage of latency during which the performance is admittedly not accurate. But instead of setting up an ideal of perfection before the work begins, instead of insisting upon an ideal of accuracy that bears no relation to the composition being studied, the compositional attitude during practice views "accuracy" as an outcome of the work, as concomitant to the final stage of performance. The final stage is faithful to the notation because the spirit of the composition cannot be properly manifested in any other terms. An "inaccuracy" that serves the spirit of the composition in the early stages of the performance has assured an "accuracy" in the final stage that is completely in accord with that spirit. By playing the composition in terms of its layers, the student has become convinced that the composer's choice of materials is the best. Any use of materials other than the composer's would produce a different composition and a less satisfactory one.

Interest in musical analysis, then, means playing the composition as a development of the background into the foreground. By redefining the significance of "accuracy," it overcomes the tyranny of "the wrong note." It does away with a sort of sense of musical sin that such tyranny induces. A sensation of defeat, of having fallen short of a preordained ideal of perfection, is responsible for most doubts about possessing musical talent. Once the student realizes that to be upset by the wrong note is to be defeated before the battle, before the qualities that make up musical talent have had an opportunity to take effect, he finds that there is room for everyone in performance and sufficient talent to accomplish its aims. To engage in performance as a developing process is to tap unsuspected resources of talent.

37 CONCLUSION

The sense that everyone has ample talent for performance follows only from the kind of definition of performance we have given in the preceding chapters. In conclusion, then, let us summarize this view of performance.

It begins with the idea that the composer, with the aid of a heritage of musical materials, builds a structure out of elements that seem to him to be mutually appropriate. He believes that others, too, will consider his choice of elements appropriate because he is convinced that they occur together in human experience. Whether he is rewarded for his structure, in money or in recognition, depends upon the value the society of his time attaches to it. Yet the value of his music and its monetary value are two different things. The value of his music lies in whatever gain is experienced by listeners from the appropriateness that he has observed and recorded. He has made certain areas of existence more understandable to them, areas which can be explored best, he believes, by musical means.

Often, the composer can present his structure, can perform, himself. But he also has the option of permitting another individual to substitute for him and the necessity of involving a group when he composes for chorus or orchestra. He will then require the intervention of notation. Again, whether these substitutes and groups are recognized or paid for their work will depend on the society they live in. But the value from their performances is once more the gain from better understanding of human experience.

Be the performer the composer, a substitute, or a group, performance is a special kind of service. To undertake it, one must believe in the increased understanding of experience that it affords. Composers and performers should be paid for their work in the same sense that other producers can sell what they and their families do not need. But since the gain from greater understanding is not as easy to recognize as the gain, let us say, from eating food, the motivation for producing performance must be deeper. The motivation must survive the period before the activity attains a condition of surplus. Initially, composition and performance are efforts of the individual to relate experience to himself. Their service is first to himself. Only later, when that service transcends his own needs, can it become available to others.

Within the total activity of music, there is greater gain to understanding from performing than from listening and greater gain from composing than from performing. The differences in gain are due to greater or lesser nearness to the sources in actual human experience. The composer is closest, the performer twice removed, and the listener thrice. Consequently, in the transmission of understanding across this network that recedes from the source, error can creep in. Verification is needed at each of the network's junctures—the composer may not have observed and recorded experience adequately; the performer may not have interpreted the notation suitably; the listener may not have been sufficiently perceptive or sensitive. How can such verification be provided? By versing oneself in performance and becoming a competent judge.

Whoever wishes to engage in music must accept the responsibility of upholding the gain to understanding that the activity affords. He must know when the composer, performer, and listener have fulfilled their functions well or ill. The acceptance of this responsibility is open to everyone because music is a universal art, and musical talent, in the wider meaning we have given it, is universally possessed. Yet the responsibility should not be lightly assumed. It demands faith in the validity of human experience and an unfailing service to increased understanding in the face of more easily demonstrable values.

NOTES

1. Pablo Casals confirms the central place of the piano as follows: "I must say I am glad I learned the piano at the very beginning. For me it is the best of all instruments—yes, despite my love of the cello. On a piano you can play anything that has been written . . . the instrument encompasses everything. That is why everyone who wants to devote his life to music should know how to play the piano." Pablo Casals (as told to Albert E. Kahn), *Joys and Sorrows* (New York: Simon and Schuster, 1970), p. 30.

2. Charles Phillips, *Paderewski* (New York: Macmillan, 1934), p. 172.

3. Paul Hindemith, *A Composer's World* (Cambridge, Mass.: Harvard University Press, 1952), p. 133.

4. The first two of these three aspects of the attack on the performer are too familiar to need documentation. Indeed, the pendulum has swung to the other extreme with a profusion of grants and commissions available to composers and with a strong emphasis on musicology in the curriculums of universities. The third aspect, formation of a psychology of music, is less familiar. But as scientific conclusions filtered to the public

through secondary, popularizing sources, it has been equally influential. Scientific investigation of performance, one small branch of the total work in psychology of music, received strongest impetus from the psychologist Carl E. Seashore (see notes, 35, 41, and 51). His conclusions about piano performance were supplemented by Otto Ortmann, *The Physical Basis of Piano Touch and Tone* (New York: Dutton, 1925); see notes 32 and 37.

5. Harold C. Schonberg describes this change. Writing of "an American school of piano-playing," he states: "Eclectic in approach, clear in outline, metrically a little inflexible, tonally a little hard, they tend to be literalists who try for a direct translation of the printed note. . . . The result is a uniformity in playing, where the general level is certainly higher than it was years ago, but where there are few peaks." *The Great Pianists* (New York: Simon and Schuster, 1963), p. 429.

6. Arthur Loesser refers to a period "beginning with the later 1920's" as "The Dusk of the Idol," a decline of interest in the previously popular pianoforte. He ascribes the decline to a variety of economic and sociological causes rather than to the emphasis on skill. He cites

the plight of piano manufacturers, the competition of the player piano and the phonograph, and changes in the attitude toward music in the home and among the younger generation. However, he adds that students of the piano still outnumber students of other instruments and also that the piano has played a surprisingly large role in the activities of popular music. *Men, Women and Pianos* (New York: Simon and Schuster, 1954), pp. 509–608, 613.

7. Alfred Einstein, *Music in the Romantic Era* (New York: Norton, 1947), p. 31.

8. Marc Pincherle makes an important distinction between virtuosity and "its exaggerated form, which has been called *virtuosoism*." "There can be virtuosity without music, there can not be, there could not have been, music without virtuosity. The whole thing is to choose as perfect examples not Lolli, Steibelt, or Kalkbrenner, but Frescobaldi, Bach, Mozart, François Couperin." The contributions of Pincherle, with whom I had the privilege of studying, are characterized by a rare and notable balance of attitude: "It would be unfair to condemn something which taken all in all is fruitful, for the abuses to which it, like everything else, is exposed." *The World of the Virtuoso* (New York: Norton, 1963).

9. Claude Debussy, *Monsieur Croche, the Dilettante Hater* (New York: Lear, 1948). These articles had the greater impact of appearing in the Paris newspaper *Figaro*.

10. Lectures by Maurice Ravel and Nadia Boulanger, *Rice Institute Pamphlets*, Vol. XIII (Houston: Rice Institute, 1926).

11. For a study of the widespread musical activity and for a constructive attitude toward the possibilities in the amateur, see Jacques Barzun, *Music in American Life* (New York: Doubleday, 1956): "Music is no private pastime tolerated in one corner of our culture, but a pervasive element of it" (p. 26).

12. Quoted by Ernest Newman, in *Wagner as Man and Artist* (London: John Lane; New York: Knopf, 1925), p. 163.

13. Sylvia Townsend Warner, "Notation," *Grove's Dictionary of Music and Musicians*, 3rd ed. (London and New York: Macmillan, 1927), Vol. III, p. 646.

14. Besides *crescendo*, other examples that illustrate the origin of notation indications in compositional processes are the triangular *staccato* mark, *con anima*, and *sostenuto*. Gustav Nottebohm, *Beethoveniana*, Vol. 1 (Leipzig: Peters, 1872), p. 106, discusses the necessity for the more trenchant, incisive significance of the triangular *staccato* mark as opposed to the circular dot. *Con anima* calls attention to a contrasting section of greater mobility and lighter mood: see Bruce Simonds, "Chopin's Use of the Term, *Con Anima*," *MTNA Proceedings*, 1948, p. 151. *Sostenuto* has the opposite meaning and applies to a contrasting section with staid movement and sober mood. Brahms, who used it frequently, treats it as if it had been temporarily added to the term covering the initial tempo; e.g., *andante* becomes *andante sostenuto*.

15. R. G. Collingwood, *The Principles of Art* (London: Oxford University Press, 1938), p. 321.

16. Alexander Wheelock Thayer, *The Life of Ludwig van Beethoven* (New

York: The Beethoven Association, 1921), Vol. 1, p. 292. See also footnote by the translator H. E. Krehbiel.

17. Regrettably, there is a tendency when evaluating achievements of the past to spread the fault that has been found with a detail to a man's entire contribution. Matthay, Cortot, and Schenker have not escaped this extension of criticism from a part to the whole. Yet the enormous influence they have had and continue to exert cannot be gainsaid. It lives on, even where unacknowledged, and nothing has appeared in their fields since their time to compare with the scope of their contributions.

18. As stated at the beginning of this section, the basic factors of Matthay's method were first defined by him in *The Act of Touch* (London: Longmans, Green, 1903). They were further clarified in *First Principles of Pianoforte Playing* (London: Longmans, Green, 1905). The quotations are drawn from these works and arranged into a summary with the aid of Matthay's own digests and tables, which he also extracted and published separately.

19. Note to Part I, *The Act of Touch, op cit.*

20. Tobias Matthay, *Musical Interpretation* (Boston: Boston Music Co., 1913), p. 21.

21. Alfred Cortot, in his annotated edition of Frédéric Chopin, *Twenty-four Preludes*, Op. 28 (Paris: Senart, 1926), p. 2.

22. Cortot, foreword to his annotated edition of Chopin, *Twelve Etudes*, Op. 10 (Paris: Senart, 1915).

23. Cortot, in his annotated edition of Chopin, *Four Ballades* (Paris: Senart, 1929), p. 19.

24. *Ibid.*, p. 20.

25. Chopin, *Twelve Etudes, op. cit.*, p. 61.

26. Heinrich Schenker, *Neue musikalische Theorien und Phantasien* (Vienna: Universal Edition, 1935), Vol. III (*Der freie Satz*), p. 24.

27. Felix Salzer, *Structural Hearing* (New York: Boni, 1952).

28. Schenker, *op. cit.*, examples 138, 5 and 153, 3a–b.

29. For a clear, concise summary of the factors in this relation, see DeWitt H. Parker, *The Principles of Aesthetics* (Boston: Silver Burdett, 1920), pp. 170–81.

30. Cortot, in Chopin, *Twenty-four Preludes*, Op. 28, *op. cit.*

31. Sir James Jeans, *Science and Music* (Cambridge: Cambridge University Press, 1961), p. 98. The gist of this quotation, stated in many different ways, may be found in many other books because it is the usual starting point for scientific discussions of performance.

32. Otto Ortmann, *The Physical Basis of Piano Touch and Tone* (New York: Dutton, 1925). Ortmann makes this common mistake, as the following quotation shows: "If A plays poetically and B does not, then, as far as the single tone is concerned A plays sounds of different intensity from those of B; and if B could play sounds of the same intensity as A, B would play just as poetically as A" (p. 171).

33. William James, *Principles of Psychology* (New York: Holt, 1890), Vol. I, p. 612.

34. M. T. Henderson, "Rhythmic Organization in Artistic Piano Performing," *Studies in the Psychology of Music*, Vol. IV (Iowa City: University of Iowa Press, 1937), p. 288.

35. M. T. Henderson, Joseph Tiffin, and Carl E. Seashore, "The Iowa Camera and Its Use," *Studies in the Psychology of Music, op. cit.*, p. 258.

36. Hermann von Helmholtz, *On the Sensations of Tone*, translated by Alexander J. Ellis (London: Longmans, Green, 1895), p. 187.

37. Sympathetic resonance is the vibration of one string in response to some other string bearing the proper relationship of frequency to it. Ortmann, in the book cited in reference 32, above, is therefore again in error when he limits sympathetic reinforcement to action of the pedals: "Since the use of this vibration form depends on either the una corda or the damper pedal, it cannot be directly influenced by the keyboard touch of the player and hence forms no exception to the general rule that the sole variations in tone through touch are intensive" (p. 122).

38. Frank Howes, *The Borderland of Music and Psychology* (London: Kegan Paul, Trench, Trubner, 1926), p. 69.

39. Carl E. Seashore, *In Search of Beauty in Music* (New York: Ronald, 1947), pp. 71–72.

40. *Ibid.*, p. 72.

41. *Ibid.*, p. 212.

42. In his *Collected Papers* (New York: Basic Books, 1959), Vol. IV, p. 184, Sigmund Freud reviews a pamphlet by the philologist Karl Abel on "The Antithetical Sense of Primal Words." Abel had stated: "In this extraordinary language (ancient Egyptian), there are compound words like 'oldyoung', 'farnear', 'bindloose', and 'outsideinside'. Man has not been able to acquire even his simplest and oldest conceptions otherwise than in contrast with their opposites; he only gradually learned to separate the two sides of the antithesis and think of the one without conscious comparison with the other" (pp. 186–187). Freud saw in these circumstances a similarity with the language of dreams. The arrangement of sensations in categories between opposites remains a significant feature of art.

43. L. N. Vernon, "Synchronization of Chords in Artistic Piano Music," *Studies in the Psychology of Music, op. cit.*, p. 311.

44. Curt Sachs, *The Rise of Music in the Ancient World* (New York: Norton, 1943), p. 108.

45. *Oxford History of Music*, Introductory Volume (London: Oxford University Press, 1929), p. 69.

46. Willi Apel, *The Notation of Polyphonic Music* (Cambridge, Mass.: The Mediaeval Academy of America, 1942), p. 199.

47. Roger Sessions, in *The Musical Experience of Composer, Performer and Listener* (Princeton, N.J.: Princeton University Press, 1950), pp. 92–99, outlines detailed and rigorous requirements for the listener. However, he views these requirements as a demand upon the listener to reach the high level of the composer's message. The direction of effort is essentially one-way, and he does not see the composer's work as fundamentally concerned with the

listener and as determined by the conditions of the listening process.

48. This relation between nursery rhymes and basic features of musical structure is further discussed in David Barnett, "Harmonic Rhythm and Mother Goose," *Music Educators Journal*, June, 1959, pp. 20–23.

49. In recent years, the term evolution has apparently lost favor as suitable for the course of music history; see Warren Dwight Allen, *Philosophies of Music History* (New York: Dover, 1962), pp. 261–85. However, in the sense in which I am using it, namely, as appropriate to the meaning of complexity, it is entirely fitting because I point out that complexity does not imply superiority. A symphony is undeniably more complex than a folksong, but both can give musical satisfaction. Further, the designation "evolutionary" is justified by the layered construction of music which superimposes one stratum upon another with increasing detail. Without the recognition that the foreground and middleground layers are more complex than the background and evolve from it, reduction by analysis would be impossible.

50. Thayer, *op. cit.*, Vol. II, pp. 290–92, quotes Beethoven's dedicatory letter and Schindler's comments.

51. "Criticism of these tests" for musical talent "has reached a fairly general agreement that they are not really tests of musical ability at all, that they are tests of aural endowment which may have quite low correlation with proved musical ability." This comment is made by Frank Howes in *Man, Mind and Music* (London: Secker and Warburg, 1948), p. 114. The definitive case in favor of talent tests was set forth by Carl E. Seashore in *The Psychology of Musical Talent* (New York: Silver, Burdett, 1919). In one of the very first reviews of this book (*Psychological Bulletin*, September, 1919, p. 354), H. G. Bishop already made the criticism that has recurred consistently: "A more serious difficulty lies in the fact that there is no convincing evidence that the sum of the elementary capacities (something that does not vary with training or age or intelligence) will combine into musical talent." James L. Mursell upheld the view that the base for judging musical ability is far broader than the tests can provide (e.g., in "What About Music Tests," *Music Educators Journal*, October, 1939, p. 16). In *Exploring the Musical Mind* (New York: Coleman-Ross, 1958), Jacob Kwalwasser, equally firm in support of the opposite point of view, held the tests to be valid.

52. Alfred Cortot, *French Piano Music* (Paris: Rieder, 1932), Vol. I, p. 40.

53. See Herbert Weinstock, *Chopin* (New York: Knopf, 1949) pp. 74–75. In fairness to Kalkbrenner, it should be added that the young Chopin was dazzled by the prospective teacher's pianism. There can be no doubt of Kalkbrenner's mastery; he simply could not recognize a divergent style.

54. Karl Leimer and Walter Gieseking, *The Shortest Way to Pianistic Perfection* (Philadelphia: Presser, 1932).

55. See David Barnett, *Living with Music* (New York: Stewart, 1944), for extensive use of compositional methods in instructing grade school children.

GLOSSARY

Appropriateness: See Canon of appropriateness.

Arpeggio: A manner of performing a chord by presenting its notes in quick, upward or downward succession. The term is derived from the Italian *arpeggiare*, meaning "to play upon the harp," and is notated by a wavy line to the left of the chord.

Asynchronization: A manner of performing the notes of a chord that includes *arpeggiation* but also permits them to be presented in any other order or way besides upward and downward succession.

Acts of comparison: A description of the essential activity in listening to music. The comparison depends on recognizing the *links* that make up *musical continuity*. These links may be as long as a phrase or as short as a motif, and by comparing one to the next the listener detects the extent of their similarity and difference. Stated another way, he detects the *rate of change* in the musical continuity.

Advantage for salience: The conditions accompanying the appearance of a note in a passage determine its *potential for salience*. When these conditions are particularly favorable and increase its potential for salience, the note is said to have an advantage for salience.

Background: One of three terms used by Henrich Schenker to explain musical structure. The background is a basic pattern that is transformed into the final form or *foreground* of the composition by *prolongation* or the activity of the *middleground*. This activity of prolongation may be compared to the production of variations upon a theme.

Cadence: The arrangement of notes at the end of a musical phrase to give the sensation of partial or complete conclusion. Analogous to punctuation.

Canon of appropriateness: The criterion that determines whether the elements of a musical composition belong together. It is derived ultimately from those perceptions in human experience that group the subjects and characteristics of nature into stable and unified patterns.

Central purpose: The expressive object to which the performer believes all of the composition's musical elements contribute. It may also be referred to as the subject of a piece of music or as the factor that gives unity to the composition's variety.

Change: See Rate of change.

Comparison: See Acts of comparison, Horizontal comparison, Vertical comparison.

Complexity: A more comprehensive term for the structure of music than Schenker's three terms *background, middleground,* and *foreground,* because it refers to each and every *layer* as a stage in constructing a musical passage. *Layer analysis,* then, is the discovery of the steps in understanding the structure of a composition. The term *complexity* is preferable because the composer could stop construction at any layer and cause it to be regarded as the final form of a composition. No one layer is considered superior to another but merely more or less complex. (See also Evolutionary complexity, Organic complexity.)

Context: The poetic image to be achieved by the performance. Akin to the *central purpose* but referring more to characteristics in nature than to musical elements. In the performer's opinion, the characteristics of the poetic image relate to characteristics in a composition and make its elements mutually appropriate.

Continuo: A standardized series of chords or succession of harmonies that underlies most musical compositions during any one musical epoch. Usually identified with the baroque period (1600–1750) and its practice of notating only the bass part and indicating the others by arabic numerals that represent intervals above the bass.

Conversance with idiom: Each person born into a musical epoch becomes familiar both unconsciously and consciously with the prevailing musical idiom or vocabulary. Most features of this idiom are too subtle to be notated in the musical score and they therefore constitute an *oral supplement* to the score.

Damper pedal: The pedal depressed by the right foot of the pianist. It raises all the dampers or felt pads at once from their position of rest on the strings, permitting them free vibration.

Deviation: A theory advanced by Carl E. Seashore, Otto Ortmann, and other psychologists to explain values used in artistic performance. According to this theory, the player first learns *regularity,* which is metronomic time, pure tone, true pitch, and even loudness. He then departs at will from such mathematical types of values, using what is called "poetic license."

Elements of structure: The term *element* is not synonymous with the term *layer,* but refers to designs or patterns of rhythm, melody, or harmony from which the layer itself is constructed.

Evolutionary complexity: The qualifying term *evolutionary,* applied to a layer of musical structure, signifies that no one layer is superior to another but merely more or less complex. It is suggested by analogy with the theory of evolution. There, species are differentiated according to degrees of complexity and not on grounds of superiority.

Foreground: One of Schenker's three terms to describe musical structure. The foreground is the final form of the composition that the action of the *middleground* has built upon the *background.*

Horizontal comparison: The term *horizontal* describes the listener's acts of comparison when he is concerned with successive *links* and detects the extent of similarity and difference as, so to speak, they pass in review before him. This horizontal view of structure, of which the perception of a sequence is one example, is concerned with the *organic* type of complexity.

Idiom: See Conversance with idiom, Musical idiom.

Instrument: See Occasional instrument, Solo instrument.

Layer analysis: The discovery of the steps in understanding the structure of a musical passage. Reduction of a passage's rhythmic, melodic, and harmonic complexity into a series of layers that are graded according to degree of complexity.

Links: Musical continuity is best compared to links in a chain, not to a flowing stream. The listener must be able to break up the continuity into *prior* and *subsequent* links, in order to compare them for similarity and difference.

Middleground: In Schenker's terms for musical structure, the process of *prolongation* whereby the *foreground* is built on the *background*.

Modal system: The system of constructing scales and the music based on them up to about the beginning of the 17th century. It consists of shifting the two half-steps to different locations within the scale. The *diatonic system* that replaced it does not shift the half-steps and instead transposes the same pattern of scale construction, thereby producing different *keys*. Use of modal scales by Debussy and Ravel and by others who followed their example did not set aside the diatonic system because it still involved keys. It was a revival of interest in modal scales—what may be termed *neo-modality*—rather than a return to a modal system.

Musical idiom: The prevailing musical vocabulary of an epoch—motifs, rhythms, melodic inflections, harmonies—together with the preferred methods of organizing it into senseful combinations.

From epoch to epoch, the idiom changes sufficiently to permit trained listeners to date music that is unfamiliar to them.

Natural salience: Nature has endowed certain musical materials with a strong *potential for salience*. For example, the octave was discovered by many nations. Man was guided in the choice of the materials of his music by their natural salience, by the way they stood out from other possible materials.

Neapolitan chord: A major triad borrowed from the second degree of the Phrygian scale and used in place of the diminished triad on the second degree of the Aeolian or minor scale. It imparts a particularly melancholy inflection.

Occasional instrument: The term suggested for instruments like the celesta and xylophone because their timbre is too characteristic to permit them to imitate the sound of other instruments.

Oral supplement: The unwritten or unnotated portion of the musical score. Those born during an epoch become conversant with the prevailing musical idiom. Too elusive and subtle to be written down in full details, it depends on an oral supplement to the score.

Organic complexity: The term *organic* is applied to that aspect of musical structure or complexity which is revealed to the listener by his acts of *horizontal comparison*. He compares the *subsequent link* with the *prior link* and detects the *rate of change* that they represent. The term *organic* is appropriate for this type of complexity because it involves perception of the interdependence of the links in the musical continuity.

Overelaboration: See Redundancy.

Pentatonic: Literally "five-note,"

and referring to a more ancient scale than the seven-note standard scale. It can be represented by omitting the fourth and seventh letters as follows C D E G A.

Performance value: Refers to the performer's utilization of pitch, intensity, duration, and timbre in creating relationships of salience out of natural and structural conditions. Requires exercise of the performer's judgment.

Poetic salience: For proper accentuation, the tones of a musical phrase must be arranged in a hierarchy of relative salience. When the performer creates a greater degree of salience than phrase recognition would demand, he has a further purpose. His object is to convey some aspect of his own state or condition. The suggested term for this greater degree of salience is poetic salience.

Potential for salience: A note's potential for salience is the sum of the endowment by nature that has made it stand out from other materials and the conditions accompanying its appearance in a passage. The performer judges this potential in arriving at his performance value.

Prolongation: Schenker's term for the activity of the middleground that builds the foreground on the background.

Prosaic salience: The normal or usual accentuation of a phrase which has no further purpose than to promote phrase recognition. It implies a more impersonal attitude, whereas poetic salience springs from a personal attitude.

Proximity: A relative term under the heading of duration. It relates the durations of successive tones from moment of entry to cessation of sound. The concept of proximity treats simultaneity as an infinite limit. The more precise the measuring device, the more clearly simultaneity is seen to be some form of asynchronization.

Purpose: See Central purpose.

Rate of change: The extent of similarity and difference between prior and subsequent links of the musical continuity. Produces an infinite number of sensations between the one extreme of smooth transition and the other of abrupt dislocation.

Redundancy: An oversupply of rhythm or melody or harmony among the elements of a passage that indicates a further or more remote purpose on the part of the composer. Thus, the typical constant insistence on the waltz bass in a waltz makes both the three-quarter rhythm and the pattern itself redundant; it becomes an accompaniment and loses priority to further purposes in the treble melody.

Regularity: A term used by Seashore as part of his theory of deviation. It refers to metronomic time, pure tone, even loudness, and true pitch. The performer is said to master such mathematical values and then to deviate from them according to the dictates of artistic license. This theory cannot be reconciled with the musical behaviour of folk musicians and children. In the latter part of this book, the term regularity is used in a different sense. There, it refers to the leeway that surrounds a notation symbol and permits the operation of the tolerance.

Salience: The player's concern with tone is not properly described as a judgment of intensity. A much more accurate term for his tonal activity is judgment of relative salience: He is vitally concerned with how much a tone stands out from or blends with other tones. (See also Advantage for salience, Natural salience, Poetic salience, Potential for salience, Prosaic salience, Salient characteristic.)

Salient characteristic: This term may refer to an outstanding feature of a tone, of a passage, or of a poetic image, and parallels may be drawn that relate all three. Thus, somber tone, the minor mode, and the slow tread of marching feet, as salient characteristics of tone, passage, and poetic image respectively, may be interrelated to produce a funeral march.

Solo instrument: An instrument possessing sufficiently flexible and and adaptable timbre to permit imitation of other instruments. Examples of such instruments are the violin, piano, and human voice.

Synthetic timbre: The mutual reinforcement of intervals in performance. Use of this factor of reinforcement as a principle for rearranging the notes of chords in imitation of the distribution of upper partials within the harmonic series. Synthesizing a timbre with the aid of actual notes instead of overtones.

Thematic timbre: The tendency of certain themes or groups of notes to recall the instruments with which they are mainly associated even when performed on other instruments. Horn-calls and fanfares are familiar examples.

Timbre: See Synthetic timbre, Thematic timbre.

Tolerance: An area or leeway of choice surrounding the notation symbol within which any performance value represents that one symbol. The materials of music are so arranged that such varied choices will not be confused with the next notation symbol in the same category.

Vertical comparison: The technique whereby *evolutionary complexity* is reduced to simpler layers. Analogous to the process of cancellation in solving fractions or to the practice of diagramming sentences. It is vertical because it can be applied to the first link of a composition without involving the next or subsequent link. It requires the listener to penetrate the more complex layers and perceive the simpler ones beneath them.